Child-Centred Foster Care

of related interest

Promoting Children's Rights in Social Work and Social Care
A Guide to Participatory Practice
Margaret Bell
Foreword by Mary John
ISBN 978 1 84310 607 4
Children in Charge series

A Practical Guide to Fostering Law
Fostering Regulations, Child Care Law and the Youth Justice System
Lynn Davis
Foreword by Christopher Simmonds
ISBN 978 1 84905 092 0

Understanding and Working with Parents of Children in Long-Term Foster Care
Gillian Schofield and Emma Ward
ISBN 978 1 84905 026 5

Understanding Looked After Children
An Introduction to Psychology for Foster Care
Jeune Guishard-Pine, Suzanne McCall and Lloyd Hamilton
Foreword by Andrew Wiener
ISBN 978 1 84310 370 7

Young Children's Rights
Exploring Beliefs, Principles and Practice
2nd edition
Priscilla Alderson
Foreword by Mary John
ISBN 978 1 84310 599 2
Children in Charge series

Fostering Now
Messages from Research
Ian Sinclair
Foreword by Tom Jeffreys, Director General, Children,
Families and Young People Directorate, DfES
ISBN 978 1 84310 362 2

The Pursuit of Permanence
A Study of the English Child Care System
Ian Sinclair, Claire Baker, Jenny Lee and Ian Gibbs
ISBN 978 1 84310 595 4
Quality Matters in Children's Services series

Child-Centred Foster Care

A Rights-Based Model for Practice

Annabel Goodyer

Foreword by Sue White

Jessica Kingsley *Publishers*
London and Philadelphia

Contains public sector information licensed under the Open Government Licence v1.0.
Figure 2.2 from Hart 1992 on p.43 is reproduced by permission
of UNICEF Innocenti Research Centre, Florence.

First published in 2011
by Jessica Kingsley Publishers
116 Pentonville Road
London N1 9JB, UK
and
400 Market Street, Suite 400
Philadelphia, PA 19106, USA

www.jkp.com

Library of Congress Cataloging in Publication Data
Goodyer, Annabel, 1952-
Child-centred foster care : a rights-based model for practice / Annabel
Goodyer ; foreword by Sue White.
p. cm.
Includes bibliographical references and index.
ISBN 978-1-84905-174-3 (alk. paper)
1. Foster home care--Great Britain. 2. Foster children--Great Britain. I.
Title.
HV887.G5G66 2011
362.73'30941--dc23
2011017936

British Library Cataloguing in Publication Data
A CIP catalogue record for this book is available from the British Library

ISBN 978 1 84905 174 3

Printed and bound in Great Britain

Contents

Foreword

Based on thorough, sociologically informed research into children's stories about being fostered, this book challenges some of the dominant theoretical and conceptual approaches to understanding children's experiences. By shifting the analytic gaze away from deficit-focused accounts of children as bundles of developmental needs, or as attachment-rich or attachment-poor entities, Annabel Goodyer manages to animate the children who informed this study. Her data flesh out those children and even give voice to those who powerfully describe having no voice. She shows how children, overwhelmed by the process and experience of 'being moved', act rationally and strategically to avoid situations or exert control over them. Some actions, such as staying away from the home all day, place them at increased risk, but they are purposeful actions nonetheless.

Goodyer reminds us that children who are fostered are social agents. They are not passive objects of state interventions made in their 'best interests', but seek, like all of us, resources to allow them to exercise their agency. Community, networks and possessions such as mobile phones feature in the children's accounts of things that helped them when they moved. Slippery concepts like 'belonging' and 'trust' are opened up to reveal complex negotiated settlements that defy prescriptive policy or practice solutions. Children carry different versions of belonging, with some identifying the foster placement as their primary belonging and some affirming that they belonged with their birth family. These settlements must be negotiated in interaction and relationship each time a child moves.

Throughout the book, Goodyer draws contrasts and comparisons with major studies of fostering, which makes this book an excellent review of literature as well as a research-informed text in its own right. Moreover, by addressing matters such as the relationship between the public and the private, children's experiences of the bureaucratic regulation of fostering, and the impact of technologies such as social networking, this book has plenty to say about practising social work in contemporary society. The accounts in Chapter 7 of children's frustrations with the regulations and decision-making in children's services strike a chord with the stories submitted to the recent Munro Review of Child Protection in England, on which I served. One story told to us was of a child who was unable to go on holiday with his foster carers because the authorisation process in the local authority was too labyrinthine and ponderous to cope with 'real time' planning for a family holiday. The child was accommodated in a respite placement instead. One rather chilling comment in this book is that children tended to attribute feeling safe in a foster home to good luck rather than good social work judgement.

However, this is not a sensationalising or nihilistic account of fostering that simply pours out atrocity stories in the name of critique. Many children had wholly enriching experiences of being fostered and most had very clear ideas about what could be done to improve the system. They are unconvinced of the merit of the dominant mechanisms of public accountability, and seem particularly irked that their private sphere is colonised by the public domain through well-intentioned initiatives and practice mantras, such as 'information sharing'. Instead, children recommend that accountability should focus on whether they are in a safe and supportive space, whether there is trust, whether they had a chance to get to know their foster carers before being forced to live with them, whether their social workers visited frequently, especially in the early days following a move, and whether they have a 'normal' family life. It is not surprising that what children want from fostering is not so far from what we all want from our own lives and homes.

In the later chapters of the book, Goodyer advances a model for professional practice in this domain. These chapters, informed as they are by an understanding of children as relating, emoting and competent beings, offer real possibilities for a way forward and for shaking up professional vocabularies about children and fostering where these have become stale.

Sue White
Professor of Social Work (Children and Families)
University of Birmingham

Acknowledgements

First and foremost I would like to thank the children and young people who have shared their experiences and thoughts with me so generously, as well as the social workers and participation workers who helped them to do so. Throughout the book, place names, children's names and some other identifying factors have been altered, but their accounts of being fostered remain unchanged.

Several people have offered considerable support to the writing of this book, in particular my children: Thomas, Katherine and Harriet Goodyer.

Finally, thanks are extended to my editor at JKP, Stephen Jones, and also to my colleague at London South Bank University, Professor Bob Broad, for comments and feedback on an earlier draft of Chapter 10. Any subsequent errors are entirely of my own making.

Introduction

Fostering is an important provider of care for children and young people in the UK who are looked after by their local authorities. This book focuses on children's own views about being fostered. It explores the ways in which children who are fostered explain their situation and the contribution that their lived experiences can make to fresh understandings about fostering. The main task of this book is to set out the argument for a child-centred approach to working with children who are fostered and to provide a child-centred practice model for fostering. The argument is premised on two understandings: first, that fostering, as by far the largest provider of placements for looked after children in the UK, is an important area of children's social work; second, that traditional understandings of fostering derive from developmental theories and focus on emotional and family relationships. I argue that being a looked after child is to be both a recipient of public welfare and also a member of a private foster family: our understandings of fostering therefore require revision to include both the private and the public welfare aspects of foster childhoods. The existent theoretical approaches to fostering, and models of social work practice drawn from these understandings, are largely incongruent with current policy and with the children's rights agenda: this book sets out a child-centred approach to fostering which aims to bring social work practice more in line with the ambitious UK policy drivers in the area of caring for looked after children.

I now turn to the structure of this book, which is divided into 12 chapters and an introduction. This introduction sets out the structure of the book, summarising the contents of each chapter, as the argument moves towards the concluding issue of how a fresh approach to fostering might support children in their achievement of better outcomes from their looked after childhoods. Chapter 1 then introduces the contexts of fostering.

The second chapter explores the evidence base of children's views about being fostered. A review of the key research studies reaches clear conclusions that, as recipients of fostering services, children and young people have views about their experiences that differ from adult assumptions about those lived experiences. The key messages from children's experiences are identified; later, in Part Three, these messages will form the basis for setting out a child-centred model of fostering practice.

Chapter 3 sets out the traditional knowledge base of fostering: this has largely relied on 'proxy accounts' of being fostered, informed by foster carers and social workers. Retrospective accounts from adults who had been fostered have been the bedrock of this knowledge base, although often they had been fostered in an era when fostering was delivered in quite different ways. As a social worker in South London in the 1970s, when 'delivering' children to a new foster home, I had to ask foster parents to sign a form agreeing to 'look after and bring up [named child] as they would their own child'. There were no foster carers or different types of foster care in those days; foster (substitute) parenting was the only identified task. Fostering has changed considerably since these times; it is now a fast-moving area of practice and recent accounts of children who are fostered at the time of being asked for their views have fresh, contemporaneous perspectives to contribute.

This is an interesting time for social work: many of the assumptions that underlie traditional social work practice have been and are being challenged. Assumptions that social workers are invariably competent and 'know best' are routinely challenged; Ruch and colleagues comment about 'the contested nature of contemporary practice, in which (for example) all "professionalism" may be questioned in terms of its assumptions about power and the locus of expertise' (Ruch, Turney and Ward 2010, p.8).

Service-user involvement in the design, delivery and monitoring of welfare services has forced a re-examination of the way some services are delivered. Groups representing black and ethnic minority service users and disabled people have forced revisions of the theoretical contexts and practice models through which social work services are delivered. As a responsive profession, we have embraced anti-oppressive practice and a social model of disability. Chapter 4 explores the way in which listening to the key messages from children and young people who are fostered forces us to re-examine the theoretical context of social work in this area. In essence, Chapter 4 suggests that an acknowledgement of the realities of delivering vital services to looked after children should be accompanied by a rights-based approach to ensuring minimum standards of care.

Part Two of this book is concerned with listening to what children and young people say about being fostered. The part begins with Chapter 5, which describes the author's own research study of children's views of becoming and being fostered, focusing on their views of moving into and between foster homes. Chapter 6 looks at data from the same study, this time looking at children's views about carers. In Chapter 7 we explore children's views about fostering and being fostered.

Part Three moves on to explore best practice in child-centred fostering. Chapter 8 sets out ways of communicating with children and young people who are fostered, including consideration of new technologies. How children can best be supported when they are fostered is the focus of this chapter. Advocacy, which includes representing children's expressed views and upholding their rights, is considered as a social work method for working with children and young people who are fostered. In Chapter 9, we explore some examples of best practice in child-centred fostering, both from within and outside the UK. New Zealand, for example, has some innovative approaches to understanding fostering: the treatment of foster children with post-traumatic stress therapies has met with some encouraging results. The aim of this chapter is to identify and disseminate some of the child-centred good practice in the care of looked after children. The inclusion of international best practice can be particularly pertinent given that many of the looked after children in the UK were born and have spent part of their childhood overseas.

Chapter 10 considers decision-making with and for looked after children. Maintaining a balance between the discharge of corporate parenting responsibilities and establishing a meaningful relationship with a looked after child or young person can be problematic: this chapter sets out best practice examples of how this might be tackled.

Selecting foster carers is key to the practice of fostering: Chapter 11 looks at the ways in which children's key messages about carers might be incorporated into current selection processes. The final chapter, Chapter 12, explores how joined-up services for looked after children might be delivered in a child-centred way. The inter-agency and inter-disciplinary nature of these services requires a reconciliation of differing practice models: the shared aim of a child-centred approach provides a credible goal for transcending individual practice models. This final chapter concludes by suggesting that child-centred fostering offers the opportunity for working towards enabling children and young people to achieve better outcomes from their looked after childhoods.

Part One
Setting out the Terrain

Chapter 1

Introducing the Contexts of Fostering

In this introductory chapter, the setting of fostering and the argument for a revision of current understandings and practice in fostering are explored. I begin by looking at the key facts about fostering and considering what constitutes a child-centred approach. There is no general agreement of what a child-centred approach is, but the basic principle involves engaging with children and their families, understanding and providing services that reflect their individual needs, and seeking and taking into account their wishes and feelings, but remaining aware that they may not yet fully understand the risks involved in their choices. A child-centred approach is therefore one that acknowledges a duty of care towards children and young people, but this is balanced with their own wishes and feelings as service users who are entitled to a responsive, individualised service. The following definition from the UK government publication *Safeguarding Children and Young People from Sexual Exploitation* (DCSF 2009a) provides a good starting point for understanding of child-centred services:

> 2.2 Action to safeguard and promote the welfare of children and young people who are sexually exploited should be child-centred and focus on the child's needs. Those working with children and young people should engage with them and their families throughout the process. The particular needs and sensitivities of girls and boys, children with a physical disability or learning disabilities, those from ethnic communities, or those for whom English is not their first language, should be reflected in the provision of services. The wishes and feelings of children and young people as well as the concerns of parents or carers should be sought and taken into account in reaching any decisions about the provision of services which affect them.

However...professionals should be aware that children and young people do not always acknowledge what may be an exploitative and abusive situation. (DCSF 2009a, p.13)

Facts and figures

Statistics concerning looked after children are available from all four countries of the UK: from the UK Government's Department for Education (for England), the Scottish Government's Education Analytical Services Division, the Welsh Assembly Government's Statistical Directorate and the Northern Ireland Executive's Department of Health, Social Services and Public Safety. Information about looked after children is collected annually from each of the 150 English local authorities and published, at aggregate level, on the UK government's information and statistical website. The figures in Table 1.1 are based on returns collected by the English Department for Education (DfE 2010) for the year ending 31 March 2010. I have here remained with data from only one of the four UK datasets.

Table 1.1 Children looked after by local authorities in England

Year	2007	2008	2009	2010
No. of looked after children	60,000	59,400	60,900	64,400
Male	33,400	33,400	34,600	36,100
Female	26,600	26,000	26,300	28,200
Age at 31 March				
Under 1	3,000	2,900	3,300	3,700
1 to 4	8,700	9,000	9,500	10,900
5 to 9	10,900	10,400	10,500	11,200
10 to 15	25,500	24,900	24,900	24,900
16 and over	11,800	12,200	12,900	13,800
No. in foster care	42,100	42,000	43,900	47,200
With 3 or more placements in year	7,600	7,000	6,800	7,000

Main categories of need pre-care				
Abuse or neglect	37,200	36,700	37,100	39,200
Absent parents	5,000	5,100	5,300	4,900
Family in acute stress	4,700	4,900	5,300	5,800
Family dysfunction	6,300	6,300	6,900	8,000
Ethnicity				
White British	44,600	43,800	44,500	47,100
Mixed: white and black or Asian	3,400	3,300	3,200	3,400
Asian or Asian British	2,300	2,600	3,000	3,200
Black Caribbean or Black African	3,900	3,700	3,600	3,700

Numbers have been rounded to the nearest 100.

Source: Department for Education (2010)

An exploration of the annual statistics gathered about English looked after children demonstrates how fostering has become increasingly important in the care of looked after children and young people. There were 64,400 looked after children in March 2010: 47,200 of those children were in foster homes. In 2009, 43,900 (73%) looked after children were looked after in a foster placement. This was an increase on the 2008 figure of 42,000.

The national UK statistics also reveal some improvement in the numbers of children and young people who have achieved some stability in their foster placement. Stability is defined as having been in the same placement for two years, a definition of stability that would not be likely to be acceptable if applied to children in the general population. Of those children who had been looked after for two-and-a-half years or more, 67 per cent had, in the past two years to 31 March 2009, lived in the same placement or their combined adoptive placement and preceding placement for two years. This percentage has increased gradually since 2005 when the percentage was 62.9 per cent. Approximately one-third of looked after children have therefore not lived in the same placement for two years. Worryingly, 10.9 per cent of looked after children had three or more placements during 2009, up from 10.7 per cent in 2009. This figure had been decreasing steadily from 13.7 per cent in 2005.

In 2009, the remaining 27 per cent of the looked after children population not in foster homes lived in a variety of placements: 6,920 children lived in residential care, mainly in secure units, children's homes, residential units or hostels; 4,100 lived with their parents; 2,500 were adopted during the year, most of whom were aged 1–4 years; and 1,900 looked after young people were living independently. The 2008 public service targets (PSAs), which are set by the DCSF, for the way in which local authorities should look after children in public care, were for 80 per cent of looked after children and young people to have 'permanency'. What these statistics reveal, however, is the wide variety of foster childhoods, from those settled in stable foster homes to the 10.9 per cent of looked after children who moved three or more times in the last year.

Children become 'looked after' for a variety of reasons: these were identified in Wilson et al.'s (2004) *Knowledge Review 5: Fostering Success*, a scoping overview of the trends in fostering research which was undertaken for the Social Care Institute for Excellence. This review suggested three main reasons. First, because the parents were unable to care for the child due to factors such as parental illness, imprisonment or homelessness. The second main reason mentioned is problematic parenting, covering issues such as neglect and abuse. The third reason is to do with problems attributed to the child's behaviour, or the child's relationship with the family breaking down for reasons associated with the child's conduct (Wilson et al. 2004).

Legal contexts

The lives of children who are fostered in public care are largely determined through the application, by social work practitioners, of statutory responsibilities to protect and look after children. These responsibilities are outlined in the Children Act (England and Wales) 1989, which was first implemented in 1991. As with all UK legislation, there is an international requirement that the Children Act complies with international human rights legislation. The key piece of children's rights legislation internationally is the United Nations Convention on the Rights of the Child 1989 (UNCRC), which was ratified in the UK in 1991 (UN 1989) and has now been agreed by all countries except the USA. It is a human rights treaty, covering children's civic, economic, family, social and educational rights. As a signatory the UK government agreed to work towards ensuring that UK children had access to the human rights listed in the convention: this compliance is monitored periodically. The UNCRC sets minimum standards for nation states to uphold; for example, to ensure that children have rights to a name and identity, to be consulted and to challenge decisions which directly affect them. In considering issues concerning any child, his or her race, ethnicity and religious and linguistic background must be taken into account. Children's rights encompass three distinct areas: protection, provision and participation (UN 1989). Amongst the rights that have particular relevance for looked after children are the following:

> Article 9(3): the right of the child who is separated from one or both parents to maintain personal relations and direct contact with both parents on a regular basis, except if it is contrary to the child's best interests.

> Article 12: the right to participation requires states parties to assure that the child who is capable of forming his or her own views the right to express those views freely in all matters affecting the child, the views of the child being given due weight in accordance with the age and maturity of the child.

> Article 16: the right to privacy. No child shall be subjected to arbitrary or unlawful interference with his or her privacy, family, or correspondence, nor to unlawful attacks on his or her honour and reputation.

> Article 20: children who cannot be looked after by their own family must be looked after properly, by people who respect their religion, culture and language.

> Article 25: the right of a child who has been placed by the competent authorities for the purposes of care, protection or treatment of his or her physical or mental health, to a periodic review of the treatment provided to the child and all other circumstances relevant to his or her placement.

> *(UN 1989, pp.4–8)*

The 1989 Children Act is broadly congruent with most of the aims of the UNCRC. Legislative changes since the UK adoption of the UNCRC and the Children Act 1989 have encouraged theoretical, policy and practice shifts in understandings of and attitudes towards children's involvement in the services that are provided for them. The UN Committee on the Rights of the Child requires signatories to the convention to report on their progress in enacting the provisions of the convention. The UK government is required to report every five years, and first did so in 1994; the UN Committee repeatedly expressed concern about such issues as the rights of asylum-seeking children, the lack of a Children's Commissioner for England and child poverty in the UK.

Some progress has now been made in this area, for example the appointment of a Children's Commissioner for England in 2004, but asylum-seeking children are still imprisoned with their parents. Previous legislative models of childhood which perceived children as passive and vulnerable, who relied on adult protection, interpretation and perceptions of their needs, have now been reviewed. UK legislation post-1989 has allowed children's own agency, perceptions and values to be considered, to some extent, within current thinking about and planning for children. However, the 49th session of the UN Committee on the Rights of Children met in March 2008 to respond to the reports from the four countries of the UK (UK Children's Commissioners 2008). The committee made many observations of areas where they hoped to see improvements before the next periodic reports in 2014. In relation to looked after children, the monitoring of children in foster and residential care (by social workers), the need to take into account children's views of their services, the provision of child-accessible complaints systems and the initiation of contact for children who are separated from their parents and siblings were all identified in the report as areas requiring improvement.

The Children Act 1989 is the key piece of legislation relating to entry into the looked after children's system in England and Wales. This is distinct from legislation in Scotland and Northern Ireland, where separate parliamentary systems provide differing legislation and provisions for looked after children, which lie outside the scope of this study. The concept of corporate parenting in the Children Act 1989 is one that recognises the rights of birth parents, but sees their responsibilities as being supplemented or shared by local authorities, in respect of looked after children and young people. This partnership between birth parents and local authority social services departments was fore-grounded in the Children Act 1989 (Fox Harding 1998). Fox Harding identified four possible value positions in child welfare services. The laissez faire position involves minimal public involvement in family life; for example, by the public sector arranging for the adoption of children who cannot live with their own families and then withdrawing to allow children to lead private lives. The second position is that of state paternalism. This understands the state as playing a major role in intervening and policing or monitoring family life. The third position, parental rights, premises that the state supports family life, by resourcing and making child-care provisions that respect the rights of birth parents. The fourth position, children's rights, involves enabling children and young people to make decisions about their lives and welfare services. Of these four positions that could have potentially influenced statutory 'corporate parenting' in England and Wales, the fore-grounding of the partnership between birth parents and local authorities effectively marginalised children's rights, relegating children to a position of having a say, rather than being listened to or being heard.

Within the provisions of the Children Act 1989 children can be removed from their parents' care, if they have been found by a court to have 'suffered significant harm or to be at risk of significant harm' (Children Act 1989, Section 31). These threshold criteria for entry into the care system via the courts are relative terms, which can vary in the way they are interpreted within and between local authorities. The decision-making that considers whether or not children are at risk is made initially at social work planning meetings, often inter-professional Child Protection meetings, and then adjudicated within the Court system. In a guide to the Children Act 1989 for social work professionals, Pizzey and Davis suggest that children are conceptualised within this Act as generally being adequately cared for within their own families (Pizzey and Davis 1996). Children are considered to be 'in need' (Children Act 1989, Section 17) of services for particular well-defined reasons, for example if they are 'at risk of significant harm' or they have a disability. Children and young people 'in need of services' are then assessed and appropriate services delivered to meet those assessed needs, for example to ensure their protection. In some cases children and young people will need to be removed to 'a place of safety' and/or 'looked after' by their local authority.

The route to becoming a looked after child in England and Wales within current legislation (Children Act 1989) is either on a compulsory basis through the Family Proceedings Courts, or by the child being abandoned or the local authority agreeing to accommodate the child voluntarily. This is usually when the birth relatives are unable to provide care, or need the support of temporary respite from caring for the child. Children may also be looked after on a voluntary basis by the local authority: in this case the parent or person with parental responsibility retains that authority in its entirety and the child has the legal status of 'being accommodated'.

Parents of children with a disability are also entitled to respite care, which is attributed to the greater burden of caring for a child with a disability (Davis and Edwards 2004). The effect of making a Care Order by a court is to give parental responsibility to the local authority, which is shared with the birth mother, fathers who are married to the birth mother and any other relative who has been granted parental responsibility, typically a resident unmarried father or a grandmother. These are two different routes of voluntary or statutory admission to care, which may merely reflect differing policies for dealing with the same set of circumstances, offering divergent roles for parental rights in planning and determining the ongoing care of looked after children and young people.

The Adoption and Children Act 2002, Part 2, made amendments to the Children Act 1989; three of these amendments have relevance for foster children. First it enabled a local authority foster parent to apply for a

Residence Order or a Contact Order if the child had lived with him or her for one year. Second, Section 118 requires local authorities to make care plans and hold reviews of plans for looked after children. Third, Section 119 of the 2002 Adoption and Children Act places a duty on local authorities to provide advocacy services for those children and young people who are looked after or leaving care who wish to make a complaint under the Children Act 1989. These provisions from the 2002 Act aimed to facilitate the participation of looked after children in the arrangements made for them, making the principle of their involvement in services mandatory.

The major implication of the Children Act 2004 for this study was the provision for a Children's Commissioner for England. The power of the English Children's Commissioner is distinct from those of the other three countries of the UK, in having a lower budget per head of the child population, in being part of a government department, the DCSF, instead of reporting directly to parliament, and in having a remit to report children's views and interests. The other three commissioners of the UK also have additional powers to safeguard children's rights (Aynsley-Green 2006).

All four commissioners jointly wrote the UK report for the UN Commission for the Rights of Children in 2008, which considered that local authorities in all four countries of the UK often did not fulfil their statutory duties towards looked after children, as the following excerpt explains:

> Local authorities in the UK should provide the same levels of support, care and protection [for looked after children] that any good parent would provide for their child. Nonetheless, authorities often fall short in their 'corporate parenting' role and do not fulfil their statutory duties. For example, the care plans of many children are not implemented and many young people approach leaving care without the pathway plan that is required by statute. (UK Children's Commissioners 2008, p.17)

Other goals of the 2004 Act are to encourage co-ordinated or 'joined-up' service provision through the appointment of Directors of Children's Services, linking education, health and social service provision into one management structure.

The Adoption and Children Act 2002 and the Children Act 2004 both modify some aspects of the 1989 Act, which remains the key legislation in children and families social work. The Children Act 2004 brings into play the policies outlined in *Every Child Matters* (DfES 2003), and implements its modernising agenda, within the arena of children and families social service delivery.

The *Care Planning, Placement and Case Review* (England) regulations of 2010 are the last piece of New Labour policy concerning looked after children. These regulations went before Parliament in March 2010. As part of the implementation of the Children and Young Persons Act 2008 and the *Care Matters* white paper, this new set of regulations and guidance came into force on 1 April 2011. This DCSF regulation revises parts of the Children Act 1989 and the earlier guidance that accompanied this Act (DCSF 2010). It aims to offer a coherent, streamlined approach to care planning and case review for looked after children, and is child-centred in its approach. The new regulations and guidance comprise four documents that set out the ways in which local authorities should carry out their responsibilities in relation to care planning, placement and case review for looked after children. It sets out principles for good social care practice with looked after children, which include a recognition that time is a crucial element in work with children and that continuity of relationships is important and attachments should be respected, sustained and developed. There is also an explicit acknowledgement that a change of home, carer, social worker or school almost always carries some risk to a child's development and welfare. The implementation of this new approach will be discussed in subsequent chapters.

Another new aspect to the Children Act Guidance and Regulations 2010 is a greater emphasis on children's participation, as the following excerpt shows.

> [Section] 1.10… When plans are being made for the child's future, s/he is likely to feel less fearful if s/he understands what is happening and has been listened to from the beginning… Where a child has difficulty in expressing his/her wishes and feelings about any decisions being made about him/her, consideration must be given to securing the support of an advocate.
>
> 1.11 There are further practical reasons for ascertaining a child's wishes and feelings during the care planning, placement and review process:
>
> - many children have an understanding of what is causing their problems and what underlies their needs;
>
> - they may have insight into what might or might not work in the context of their current circumstances and environment;
>
> - they often know what sort of support they would most value and be able to access…
>
> 1.12 The child's views as expressed should always be discussed, recorded and given due consideration before a placement decision is made, at every review meeting and at case conferences.
>
> *(DCSF 2010, p.4)*

In this way, the legal and policy framework provides the structure, in England and Wales, within which children and young people should be looked after in public care. There are concerns, however, including that of the English Children's Commissioner, that local authorities in the UK often fall short of their statutory responsibilities towards looked after children (UK Children's Commissioners 2008).

The case studies

Listening to children's views about being fostered is the first stage of working in partnership with children who are fostered. Their collected views provide the ideological framework for practice, in a move towards a theory base that recognises children's rights. The sheer variety of looked after childhoods that are experienced by the 60,000 children and young people in the UK is not always apparent from the current knowledge base. To illustrate the variety and complexities of those childhoods in a child-centred way, the following three case studies are used. First, case study 1 is an example of the type of placement where children said that they belonged to their foster family and thought that they would remain as a member of that family into adulthood. George was relatively well settled in a foster placement that offered him a sense of belonging. The second case study is an example of a child who was reasonably settled with her current foster carer, but who saw herself as belonging with her birth family. Alicia has lived in several placements during her care career, but hopes that her current family will offer her permanence. The final case study is that of a transient young person, who had little trust in foster carers or her birth relatives and who had moved placements frequently. Eleanor has experienced a turbulent care career and had difficulty in trusting carers and in achieving a stable childhood.

Case study 1: George

George is a 14-year-old white English boy. He has been looked after by the Metropolitan Borough of Greenbook for the last six years. George has never met his father and his name does not appear on George's birth certificate. His mother has a long-term history of substance misuse. George is the second of her five children, all of whom have been removed from her care. His 17-year-old half-sister has returned to the family home and is known to the local youth offending team. His younger half-sister lives with her paternal grandmother and the two youngest boys have been adopted from care, against his mother's wishes.

George has been fostered by the McCauley family for the last four years. Since leaving his mother's care, he initially lived with a family friend for six months, whilst his mother was in rehabilitation. When she relapsed into heavy drinking, George was moved to a foster family, whilst long-term carers were sought. After 18 months he moved to a rural area to live with the McCauleys. He is now happy and settled, although at first he did find village life quite a shock. He sees his long-term future as part of this family.

Although the care of looked after children is supposed to be reviewed every six months, George's last review was over a year ago. He dislikes reviews: they make him feel 'unnormal' and he does not want to talk about his birth family in front of strangers or indeed have his private affairs written down and sent to his school, birth mother and others. If George wants contact with his siblings, he asks his foster mother to arrange it with the social worker. He phones his mother very occasionally, but if she is drunk he only speaks to her very briefly.

The London borough who look after George placed him with the McCauleys as they were unable to find local carers. The McCauleys are carers from a private agency: the fostering rates are four times that paid to the borough's own foster carers. There are concerns about the placement which were reported by the current child and family social worker, who is a student on placement. Membership of the Freemasons is banned for employees of Greenbook Local Authority; George has, however, told his social worker that when he is 18 he will join the local Freemasons' group, which his foster father and older foster brothers belong to. Otherwise, the student is pleased with George's progress: he is doing well in a middle stream at his comprehensive school and wants to be an electrician. This ambition is supported by his carers who have arranged some holiday work experience for him with a local electrician who is a family friend.

Case study 2: Alicia

Twelve-year-old Alicia has been looked after by the Metropolitan Borough of Ardvaark on several occasions, due to her mother's mental ill-health. Alicia, her 18-month-old brother Ben and her mother are black British, from a Caribbean background. Mrs Dianova has become increasingly isolated from her family and friends, who have been alienated by her unpredictable outbursts and non-communication during long periods of depression. Alicia has had considerable absences from school: at times she was neglected and her current admission to care was initiated by neighbours' concerns that Alicia was foraging for food in the debris from the local market. Alicia once spent a year in foster care and has had three shorter admissions during her mother's hospital admissions. After Ben's birth Mrs Dianova had support from his father, who has now ended the relationship and moved away. Mrs Dianova has been in a psychiatric hospital for the last six months and both children are placed together with the Smythe family.

Alicia feels happy staying with the Smythe family; she is enjoying the freedom from having to look after her mother and baby brother. This was planned as a short-term placement: Alicia and Ben moved there after two weeks in an emergency placement that she claims was 'disgusting' due to poor hygiene, junk food and the foster carer insisting that Alicia had to undertake all of Ben's care including the night feeds. Alicia has now moved schools, because the journey back to her previous secondary school took two hours in rush-hour traffic. Mrs Smythe considers that Alicia fits in well with her family and has enrolled her in dance and singing classes which Alicia is enthusiastic about.

Contact with her mother is weekly: sometimes it goes well, but at other times there is little communication between them, particularly if Ben is asleep. Alicia says she knows how her mother will be 'by her eyes and whether she starts carrying on as soon as she get there'. Alicia just wants her mother's health to improve so that she can return home and their lives will get back to normal.

The local authority is still undertaking assessments before making plans for Alicia and Ben. They had not anticipated that Mrs Dianova's hospital admission would last so long and are concerned about the realities of the children's previous care and apparent neglect. Mrs Smythe would be willing to keep Alicia as a long-term foster child, but not Ben. Her own children are all at school and she no longer wants to care for infants or give up her part-time job.

Case study 3: Eleanor

Eleanor is a 17-year-old white British young woman. She dresses as a Goth, with dark hair, dramatic make-up and facial studs. Eleanor was born when her mother was 15 and Eleanor was largely cared for by her grandmother. When her mother left the family home with a new partner, 3-year-old Eleanor remained behind in her grandmother's care. Eleanor has been looked after by Bluebook County Council for the last nine years, following the death of her grandmother. Her mother lives locally with her younger, 7-year-old daughter. Eleanor visits sporadically, but has an uneasy relationship with her mother and her mother's current partner.

In total Eleanor has had over 30 different foster placements. The longest lasted for 18 months and the shortest for half a day. Eleanor ran away from several placements, she says, because she didn't trust the carers, and she was asked to leave others due to behavioural issues. She feels uncomfortable living in a home with men she does not know and trust. She does not keep in contact with any of her previous carers, but has some long-standing friendships with two girls from her primary school.

In her current placement Eleanor is living with a benign, elderly widow in a large flat opposite the railway station in the middle of her home town.

Eleanor and Mrs Smith seem to get on quite well: they watch some daytime television together until noon and then Eleanor takes off for the day, letting herself in late at night. She attends a college course in visual arts three days a week. Mrs Smith is trying to teach her cooking and budgeting, in an informal manner. This placement is planned to last until Eleanor reaches 18 and becomes eligible for the tenancy of a housing association flat.

These case studies have attempted to provide an introduction to the diversity of fostering experiences. Looked after children are not a homogeneous group; the reasons they become looked after fall into different categories of need, the length of time they spend in care varies and the types of foster home they find themselves in are diverse. Some enjoy a stable childhood with committed and able foster carers, some (40%) return home within six months, many transfer between foster homes in a planned way every two to three years (Sinclair 2005) and others (10.9%) have three or more placements in a year. The wider range of children's experiences will become apparent from their accounts in Chapters 4 to 8.

Chapter summary

This chapter has introduced the topic of fostering, stressing its importance as the major placement provider for looked after children and young people. Key legislation for looked after children and young people in the UK was identified as the United Nations Charter for the Rights of Children (1989) and the UK Children Act 1989. As a signatory to the UNCRC, the UK government's compliance with children's rights set out in this treaty are monitored every five years. This is a powerful driver for enhancing children's rights. Following repeated criticisms of the way in which asylum-seeking children in the UK can be imprisoned with their parents, the UK government finally announced an end to this practice in April 2011. There are practice implications for fostering in this change: many of these children will now require public care as an alternative.

Both the United Nations Charter for the Rights of Children (UN 1989) and the UK Children Act 1989 have enhanced children's rights in the UK. This has encouraged theoretical, policy and some practice shifts in understandings of and attitudes towards children's involvement in their services. The aim of this book is to contribute towards enhancing children's rights within fostering provision.

Three case studies were employed to illustrate the very different ways in which being fostered can have an impact on children's lives: these case studies will be revisited periodically throughout the book and in the concluding chapter.

Chapter 2

The Theoretical Approach

The task of this chapter is to look at the theoretical approach taken by social work and how this shapes our approach towards the subject of fostering. The theoretical approach is here understood as the explanation and understanding of fostering. The theoretical understandings of and attitudes towards children's involvement in child and family social work services has largely remained unchanged, despite the enhancement of UK children's rights brought about by the United Nations Charter for the Rights of Children (UN 1989) and the UK Children Act 1989. It draws on developmental psychology, from a position that considers children as developing, unfinished beings (Durkheim 1911; Mayall 2002). My central argument is that the use of an alternative theoretical approach from the sociology of childhood, one that conceptualises children as competent social beings, has relevance for the study of foster children. This theoretical perspective facilitates the additional consideration of issues such as children's human rights: not just those rights concerned with provision and protection, but also those of participation (UN 1989). It supports a model of social work practice as working with children and young people and upholding their rights. A broader, sociological approach also creates congruence between understandings of fostering and the current UK statutory and policy contexts, which emphasise children and young people's participation in their care.

As well as borrowing ideas from the sociology of childhood, in order to look at fostering from a different perspective, concepts from other academic disciplines are considered. For example, the concept of an overlap between public and private spheres was developed within the sociology of health and feminism. It is here suggested as an analytical device for considering foster children as members of private families but at the same time as recipients of public welfare services. These approaches together are employed to understand the complex lives of children who are fostered.

Child and family social work

As noted above, fostering is a statutory service, whose structures and regulations are prescribed by policy and legislative frameworks, but which is delivered by social work professionals and foster families. In essence, whilst social policy and the legislation based on those policies provide the context through which fostering services are provided, child and family social work is concerned with the interpretation and implementation of those laws and policies: it uses them to determine and shape the delivery of fostering services.

As an academic area, social work is, relatively speaking, an emerging academic discipline which draws on several theoretical approaches: understandings of how people progress through the life cycle, inter-professionalism, evidence-based practice and anti-discriminatory practice (Howe 1987; Payne 1997). The four main settings of social work are: mental health, vulnerable adults, disability and child and family (DOH 1999). Each strand of social work also separately draws on additional theoretical frameworks from which to interpret their service users' lives and to inform social work interventions. Child and family social work, which sees itself as positioned in a broad, inter-professional and evidence-based paradigm of children's services, has largely drawn upon a psychological frame of reference, where children are considered through the lens of developmental psychology.

Although some children's services departments now encourage children's participation, this is often interpreted as a consumer feedback process (Thomas and O'Kane 1999), conducted via adult methods of communication such as lengthy, formal meetings. Rather than children's participation being an integral part of the decision-making process, it is an added-on complexity, delivered by a separate part of children's services. Child and family social work practice remains preoccupied by the two concepts of protection and provision for children and with problematising parenting and child development: poor parenting is identified as the main cause of failure to achieve good outcomes for children. Social policy, however, acknowledges the relationship between social factors and children's development, for example with a clear impetus to address child poverty. Bullock (2006), in an appraisal of corporate parenting, suggests that the lack of integration between national welfare policies for looked after children on the one hand, which also includes concepts of participation, and the procedures and practices of children's services on the other hand, can be understood as what the system is supposed to be about and what it is actually about (Bullock 2006).

Psychological developmental theories

The consideration of children through the lens of developmental theory originated as a twentieth-century European phenomenon. Durkheim, a French sociologist and a founding father of sociology, positioned children as 'becomings', not yet full citizens, but progressing or developing towards citizenship. '[Childhood is] a period of growth, that is to say the period in which the individual, in both the physical and moral sense, does not yet exist, the period in which he is made, develops and is formed' (Durkheim 1911, p.15).

In an exploration of how the capacity to care develops in children, Hollway identified three types of developmental approaches: first, 'foundational' accounts that assume that 'babies have real limitations that change over time with experience' (2006, p.18); second, constructionist accounts which demonstrate how differing opinions or models of childhood are understood to shape children's lives as passive beings; and third, those that are critically realistic. Using Hollway's typology, most of the developmental theories currently drawn upon in child and family social work could be described as foundational. Foundational developmental models are varied, but they all start from a normative viewpoint that children should develop through stages at particular ages, before achieving the full status of adulthood (Thomas 2002). Debates in the area of developmental theory have traditionally centred around whether genetic or environmental factors are the greater influence on children's individual progression through the requisite stages, and also whether or not developmental stages are linear and progressive (Bowlby 1969; Durkheim 1911; Erikson 1982).

Developmental theories dominated consideration of children and their care for the second half of the twentieth century. From the 1950s until the 1990s, there was a general acceptance within child-care fields that developmental theories were the main ways in which children's experiences and family lives could be understood. Mayall, in a 1984 sociological study concerned with the uses mothers made of healthcare, noted the prevalence of developmental theory: 'You could say that the child development industry has cornered the market on knowledge about children' (Mayall 1984, p.129).

In 1936 Piaget described the progress made by children as they mature into adulthood (Piaget 1936). Beginning with the sensory stage when they rely on their senses, and then a pre-operant stage with an emergent ability to reason, children develop through a series of cognitive stages. By seven years old they are considered to be able to manage logical thinking, in the concrete operational stage, before developing the ability to abstract and deal with complex ideas at the post-12 year operational stage. Later Erikson (Erikson 1982) purported that children at each stage of their development face a series of tasks that they have to negotiate before achieving adulthood.

Attachment theory is a developmental theory which claims that the quality of the maternal bond which children form with their mothers in early infancy is the foundation for later development (Bowlby 1969). Bowlby was the founding father of attachment theory, maintaining that infants first establish strong attachment with their primary caregiver, who will provide the infant with security and protection, whilst the infant explores his or her environment. This attachment is considered measurable, through observation, as the following extract explains:

> observation of how a very young child behaves towards his mother, both in her presence and especially in her absence, can contribute greatly to our understanding of personality development. When removed from the mother by strangers, young children respond usually with great intensity; and after reunion with her, anxiety or else unusual detachment. (Bowlby 1969, p.3)

Developing Bowlby's concept of attachment theory, Ainsworth *et al.* (1978) categorised attachment into three types: secure, avoidant and resistant. A child's attachment behaviour is assessed by means of 'The Strange Situation Test', when a mother is observed with her child; she then leaves the room and later returns. Within this model, the secure type of attachment is considered to be demonstrated when an infant seeks protection or comfort from his or her mother on her return and receives care consistently. The avoidant type is when the infant tends to pull away from his or her mother or ignores her when she returns. The resistant type is when the infant tends to stay close to his or her mother on her return, but does not seek comfort.

In addition to attachment theory, resilience theory and ecological theories are psychological developmental theories which are emergent within child and family social work practice. Ecological theory considers that a child is located within his or her family and the family within a broader context of extended kin, social networks and community. A model of assessment relying on ecological theory is the *Framework for the Assessment of Children in Need* (DOH, DfEE and Home Office 2000). One of the key dimensions of this assessment is the capacity of the parent to meet the child's needs.

Attachment theories have been highly influential (Crawford and Walker 2003) and remain the dominant theoretical approach within child and family social work, particularly in assessing the quality of parental and caring relationships for looked after children (Howe 1999; Schofield *et al.* 2000).

Other explanations of children's needs

Resilience theory is a psycho-social theory of need, which seeks to establish the factors that help to make individual children resilient to adverse experiences. It acknowledges children's agency and individuated responses to stress (Tisdall *et al.* 2006), and considers the ways in which some children do well in adverse situations (Gilligan 2001; Rutter 1999). It has been described as a list of protective factors that are deemed necessary for increasing the chances of children in need to achieve good outcomes (Cleaver, Unell and Aldgate 1999; Sinclair 2005). In fostering, it has been applied in judgements about what foster children need in order to achieve a good life. Resilience theories include aspects of ecological theories (Olsson, Folke and Berkes 2003) and also of attachment theories, as Sinclair (2005) explains below. In a review of fostering research, Sinclair identifies that for looked after children most of these lists of resilience factors include 'the presence of a good attachment, the opportunity to make a new start and a good educational experience' (Sinclair 2005, p.51).

Maslow's hierarchy of needs is a relevant model for thinking about some of the experiences reported by foster children. It is an understanding of behaviour that has been used with adults within psycho-social settings. Within this model, achieving one's individual potential is the highest need, but to achieve this one needs to have all the lower needs addressed first, beginning with basic needs such as shelter (see Figure 2.1).

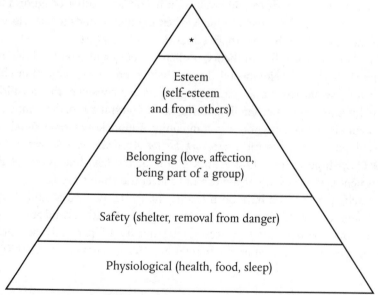

Note: * on the model is self-actualisation, or the achievement of individual potential.

Source: Adapted from Maslow (1970)

Figure 2.1 Maslow's hierarchy of needs

This model contrasts with developmentalism, affording differing priorities for achieving successful outcomes for children, for example by determining belonging as a pre-requisite for achieving academic success. This model facilitates understandings of children as people in the here and now, rather than 'becoming' people. Maslow's hierarchy of needs purports that meeting one's physical needs, the need for safety, feeling loved and having good self-esteem are all pre-requisites to achieving self-actualisation or achieving one's goals. This concept therefore has particular attraction for the consideration of the lives of foster children, whose reported experiences can include the lack of a sense of belonging or feeling of safety, as we shall see in Chapter 7.

Developmental models in social work practice

In considering the way in which developmental theory has impacted on social work, the construction of children as not yet citizens with rights, but as 'becomings' (Durkheim 1911), or future citizens, is key. Other constructions of children are employed in some aspects of child and family social work, for example children as victims or potential victims in child protection or safe-guarding practice. Attachment theory is, however, the theoretical context through which understandings about foster children are reached, as the following extract from Schofield's (2000) study of long-term fostering opines:

> Making and defending decisions in individual cases can and should draw on evidence from research, but such a defence is significantly more persuasive if it also draws on evidence drawn from theory... For children growing up in foster-care, that theoretical model must inevitably be developmental. In order to understand children who have come from situations of family adversity...it seemed appropriate to use attachment theory. (Schofield *et al.* 2000, p.2)

Developmental theories can be considered as central to the social work theory base: they form one of the five compulsory subjects on social work qualifying curricula (DOH 1999). The study of human growth and development, law, social work skills, social work interventions and inter-professional social work practice are the prerequisites for a qualification in social work. In policy relating to children, social workers with expertise in child development are considered essential for transforming the lives of looked after children (DfES 2006).

Colton, Sanders and Williams (2001), in a mainstream child and family social work practice handbook, differentiate between the social work task of being responsible for a child's welfare and advocating on behalf of a child. This distinction illustrates the way in which looked after children are largely positioned in child and family social work as the objects of concern, rather than subjects of concern. Butler-Sloss's landmark identification of children's agency, in her report of the inquiry into child sexual abuse in Cleveland, was summed up when she remarked that 'the child is a person, not an object of concern' (Butler-Sloss 1988). Since that ruling, there have been attempts from outside the social work profession to move social work practice on from this preoccupation with children as potential or actual victims in need of provision and protection, to a position that recognises their opinions and participatory rights.

Social work has been reliant on psychological understandings of 'normality' in children's development and behaviour. Although this universalism has been challenged in other fields by a consideration of diversity in childhoods (Woodhead 1997), this has only recently been challenged within child and family social work (Winter 2006). This narrow 'normative' approach, with its attendant expectations for 'appropriate' parenting, can result in missing opportunities for working in partnership with children and families who may have differing styles of child care.

Children's relationships with foster carers have been traditionally viewed through psychological perspectives. Models derived from both developmental and attachment theories are also used in fostering and adoption practice to understand and assess children's family membership, relationships and behaviour and to review their progress (Crawford and Walker 2003). This enabled a lack of attachment between a foster child and foster family to be attributed to poor early (birth) parenting. Children could be either viewed as having transferable healthy attachments and therefore suitable for adoption, or to be too damaged by poor early attachment to settle in a substitute family (Fahlberg 1991, 2004). The following two excerpts, from a textbook intended as an introduction to psychology for foster carers by Guishard-Pine and colleagues who work within clinical psychological support services for looked after children, illustrate this point:

> Attachment theory will be, in some shape or form, at the root of judgements made about the child's relationship with parents and at the root of possible future predictions about the child's ability to form different relationships. (Guishard-Pine, McCall and Hamilton 2007, p.44)

> [Understanding] may seem painfully obvious as a requirement of any foster carer for a child who comes into their care, but given that children with attachment difficulties can be very hard to relate to, they are often not only 'difficult to handle' but hard to like and hard to understand. (Guishard-Pine et al. 2007, p.55)

To summarise, foundational developmental theories have a disproportionate significance in the consideration of the lives of fostered children. Despite a changing legal and policy context which advocates children's rights (Children Act 1989; UN 1989), child and family social work has yet to re-negotiate the status of children according to a model that works in partnership with children as recipients of public services and as people with rights. What is required is a practice model that draws on understandings of children and young people as having entitlements to human rights, in particular the rights to a private, stable family life. A rights-based social work practice model, an alternative to the developmental model, has the potential to position social work with children and young people who are fostered in a more equal partnership, in order to ensure that their rights are upheld.

Critique of developmental theory and models for fostering

Within social work there have been few challenges to the dominance of psychological developmental theories. However, four main criticisms of developmental theories and the social work practice models derived from them can be identified: the lack of acknowledgement of cultural variation in understanding childhoods, that they appraise looked after children on a deficit model, that they fail to acknowledge children as having participatory rights, and finally an acknowledgement that their lack of consideration of children's agency may inhibit broader understandings of childhoods. Whilst there are attempts to take on board these criticisms and other approaches within social psychology, these attempts do not appear to have yet been taken up in the academic discipline or practice of social work, with the notable exception of Karen Winter's work about the participation rights of looked after children (Winter 2006).

First, criticisms of developmental theories often suggest that child development is highly individual (Honey and Mumford 1992) with concepts of 'normalcy' being unhelpful, or that it is culturally specific (Penn 2005). Accusations of cultural imperialism have been levelled at Piaget and other developmental theorists (Penn 2005) for generalising from particular cultural child-rearing practices. Developmental theories that perceive childhood in a universalistic manner, as a series of stages that children progress through, are also challenged from a position that acknowledges diversity and complexity in childhoods (Woodhead 1997). Within developmental psychology, and also in sociology, there are well-established critiques of attachment theory, including that of Rogoff (2003), who maintains that family relationships differ according to dominant cultural patterns, with carers other than the birth mother providing infant care within some family structures. Hollway distinguishes between the biological mother and 'maternal care' provided by others, focusing on babies' experiences of both types of care (Hollway, Lucey and Phoenix 2007). This approach suggests that a broader pattern of infant care practices should be evaluated and considered in a complementary rather than a competitive manner.

Second, foundational developmental theories can be seen to assess looked after children according to a deficit model. Use of foundational developmental theories positions looked after children as both 'damaged and complex', and suggests that their adverse experiences require particular therapeutic and insightful interventions, from skilled and committed adults (Colton *et al.* 2001; Thomas 2005). The appraisal of looked after children on a deficit model can deny them their participatory rights. In an overview of looked after children's participation in health and education services, Winter (2006) highlights five aspects of the way in which developmental models have negative consequences for securing the participation rights of looked after children: developmental psychology presents children as passive, it focuses on their shortcomings, it denies individual capabilities, it construes children as adults in the making and it therefore tends to deny that they have the capacity to participate. It is argued here that these critiques not only have relevance for the consideration of looked after children in the health and education fields, but are also applicable when considering the participation rights of children in the provision of child and family social work. Attachment theory is the theory through which children's capacity to form an attachment to, or bond with, a substitute family is largely understood within adoption and fostering practice.

Third, criticisms of attachment theories suggest that a preoccupation with maternal relationships marginalises other factors such as genetic pre-disposition, sibling status, differing cultural child-rearing practices and peer group influence. Hollway, for example, criticises attachment theory for omitting the impact of sibling status on child development (Hollway 2006). Harris (1998) posits that parents are not solely responsible for their child's development, since nature has a strong influence that is socially mediated by parents. Gonzales *et al.* (1996) consider that community and peer group influence can also be key in such factors as criminal behaviour, as well as parental relationships.

Fourth, conceptualisations of children and childhoods solely informed by foundational development largely overlook social factors, such as poverty, cultural influences on gender roles and poor housing. They also inhibit explanations that take account of children's lives and agency.

To summarise, there are several critiques to developmental approaches in child and family social work. By focusing on foundational concepts of 'normality', other ways of looking at childhood are overlooked, namely understanding how children's lives are shaped by current contexts, the different strengths and difficulties of particular childhoods, and how, as agents, children have capabilities to contribute to their own lives.

The sociology of childhood

Whilst social work is concerned with developing practices that seek to influence the life course, sociology is primarily concerned with ways of understanding social structures and the lived experiences of individuals within those structures (Pierson and Thomas 2002). Sociological insights provide social work with opportunities for thinking outside of the developmental models with which it has been preoccupied.

The sociology of childhood emerged as a distinct sub-discipline of sociology in the UK during the 1990s with the publication of James and Prout's edited volume *Constructing and Reconstructing Childhood* in 1990. The origins of the sociology of childhood lie in Scandinavia and Northern Europe (Thomas 2002, p.18), with key works by Qvortrup (1987) from Denmark, Solberg and Vetsby (1987) and Solberg (1990) from Norway, and Alanen (1988) and Dencik (1989) from Finland, all predating James and Prout's publication. In the UK, Jenks (1996), James and Prout (1997), James, Jenks and Prout (1998) and Mayall (2002) have further developed this paradigm.

Six main components of the sociology of childhood were set out by James and Prout (1990, 1997). First, the notion that childhood is a social construction: it is seen as a culturally determined set of expectations and roles. Second, children are not simply biologically determined: physical immaturity alone does not shape the lives of all children in the same way and at the same life course moment. Children's capacity for social competence and their perceived physical abilities can vary and depend on familial and cultural expectations. Third, childhood is a feature of social structure: childhood and children's lives are worthy of study in their own right. Fourth, children are not merely passive recipients of adult values and knowledge; they have agency, participating in the construction and determination of their own lives. Children also construct their own meanings and understandings about their lived experiences. The fifth component is that the study of childhood links to a political agenda. Children, like many other minority groups, lack the political power to change their own lives (Mayall 1996). Last, the sociology of childhood suggests particular ways of conducting research with children: namely the use of methods that provide children with opportunities to describe their worlds and cultures (Christensen and James 2000).

In the 1990s the sociology of childhood (James and Prout 1990) was based on a perspective informed by social constructionism, which challenged the functionalism of Talcott Parsons, which had been introduced in the 1950s. He had understood the nuclear family as a response to the needs of industrialised societies, both as a provider of mobile labour, but also as a regulator of adult behaviour and as a means of socialising children (Parsons and Smelser 1956).

The gendered division of labour detailed by Parsons was the subject of subsequent sociological debate in the 1960s (Berger and Luckman 1967).

In the 1970s feminist thinkers focused on child care as a burden which restricted the economic and social position of women (Greer 1970; Oakley 1974). Childhood was perceived both as a biological state of physical dependency, but also as a social position or category and a permanent component of the social order (Mayall 2002). For most children, childhood is a time of protection and opportunity (Mayall 1984), but not for all children. Social conditions and the capabilities of the adults on whom they depend shape children's lives. Mayall (2002) considered children as agents in social relations, and children as a social group who are fundamentally implicated in social relational processes. In developing the sociology of childhood through a recognition of children's agency, responsibilities and contributions, Mayall also contributed to the children's rights debate. Using observations of children's own understandings of themselves as dependants who have to obey adults, and who identify power as lying with adults, she argued that children form a minority social group, a category of persons who lack power. By consideration of children as people, whose experiences are structured by gender, generation, ethnicity and class, Mayall positions children as active members of society (Mayall 2002).

Mayall (2002) distinguishes between three types of sociology of childhood. First, the sociology of children, which seeks to understand the lived experiences of children and focuses on the children's agency. Second, the deconstructive sociology of childhood that claims discourses about childhoods facilitate an understanding of childhoods as locally defined. The third type is the structural sociology of childhood, where children are conceptualised as a social group within societies, with interests and rights. Of these three definitions, this study is located within the first of Mayall's types, the sociology of children, with foster children's own views on their experiences considered as the main focus of the study. This thesis takes the position that children are reliable commentators on their lived experiences and their foster childhoods.

Understandings of children as a minority group (Mayall 2002) are reinforced by studies of particular childhoods that deviate from normative understandings of children as a protected group of 'becoming' adults (Durkheim 1911). Through consideration of street children, child carers, cyber children, child soldiers, child abuse and child crime in the field of social sciences, Wyness (2006) claims that these childhoods may challenge the current western understanding of childhood by demonstrating children's competencies, responsibilities, resilience and agency. Wyness positions children as a minority group in need of understanding and support from sympathetic adults. By conceptualising the agency of children in society,

Corsaro (2004), a US sociologist of childhood, suggests that the sociology of childhood provides an alternative to traditional models. Post-modernist perspectives adopted by Swedish researchers in the 1990s viewed children as co-constructors of knowledge, identity and culture (Dahlberg, Moss and Pence 1999). These perspectives exist both within and between academic disciplines, with children recognised as having experiences worthy of separate attention within, amongst others, the sociology of childhood (Mayall 1994), the anthropology of childhood (Toren 1999) and children's education (Dahlberg *et al.* 1999).

Children and young people who are fostered occupy distinctive childhoods, with lived experiences that cannot be fully understood by looking through the lens of developmental psychology. I have argued that a developmental perspective focuses on the assumed passivity and deficits of looked after children and overlooks their own competencies, responsibilities, resilience and agency. The sociology of childhood can therefore be considered as offering a useful model for the consideration of the wider lives of looked after children, a model which offers a credible alternative to the current dominance of foundational development theories.

Private and public

Alternative approaches for explaining looked after childhoods could include the use of a theoretical model that identifies how the private and the public domains of fostering intersect and overlap. It illustrates how the public and private come together in children's lives. Feminist thinkers first intersected the boundaries between the male dominated public domain and the private domain occupied by women. Stacey (1988) analysed divisions of labour in health care and the home from a feminist perspective. She showed how the male-dominated paid domain of hospital health care had its counterpart in the unpaid female care within the domestic domain. She showed how public funding, such as attendance allowances, provided for some types of health care to be carried out privately within the home. These services occupy an intermediate zone, where the domestic and public domains intersect: '[where] the unthinking [and unrecorded] consequences of male-dominated health and welfare policy disadvantage the unpaid carers, be they male or female' (Stacey 1988, p.209).

This concept was applied within the sociology of childhood by Mayall, who also understood the division between public and private domains as being extended to include an 'intermediate' domain (2002, p.173). Mayall, in her attempt to theorise the contributions of children, used data from her previous studies with children to support this claim:

> The intermediate domain provides a conceptual space for understanding the complexities of relations between the public and the private in highly developed welfare states – it provides a means of analysing intersections of state and family; it provides a tool for dissolving the notion of two opposed domains, and of studying how far 'lay' and 'professional' knowledge, goals and practices affect each other. (Mayall 2002, p.174)

This intermediate domain lies between private and public domains, where children and work that is traditionally viewed as women's work, such as teaching, nurturing and child care, can be considered to cross both domains. The intermediate zone is here understood as a device that can facilitate understanding of the lives of foster children. Nutt, in a study of foster carers, positioned foster children in an overlap between public and private domains (Nutt 2006). In contrast to Nutt, I position foster childhoods, rather than foster children, in the intermediate domain. Whilst fostering has been seen to take place in the private domain, with foster carers seen as substitute families, it is however shaped in the public domain. Foster children are recipients of public welfare and in (partial) control of the state in the role of corporate parents.

Within the social work discipline the two domains of public and private are conflated, thus confusing practices which are over-dependent upon theories associated with the private (development) domain with those which are directed towards the public roles of social work, such as achieving good outcomes through corporate parenting. Social policy goals of enabling children to become economically active citizens when they reach adulthood are largely understood through development theories, with poor parenting identified as the main cause of failure to achieve good outcomes for children, the private domain failing to deliver for the public domain. This book seeks to explain the ways in which the intersection of private and public domains shapes the lives of foster childhoods.

Children's rights and participation

The concept of children as citizens with rights is highly relevant to this study. The participatory rights set out in section 12 of the UNCRC (UN 1989) were interpreted in England by the Children and Young People's Unit (CYPU) of the Office of the Deputy Prime Minister as a policy to involve children in being heard, as this extract states: 'We want to hear the voices of young people, influencing and shaping local services; contributing to their local communities; feeling valued; being treated as responsible citizens' (CYPU 2001, p.27).

Distinctions within the concept of participation can be made through the use of a typology or model of participation (Arnstein 1969). This relates to levels of participation and power-sharing, identifying the difference between the aim of a policy of participation and the reality as experienced by those who participate in the design, delivery or monitoring of services. Arnstein's ladder of participation was further developed by Hart (1992) to apply to children and young people's participation in adult decision-making, as Figure 2.2 illustrates.

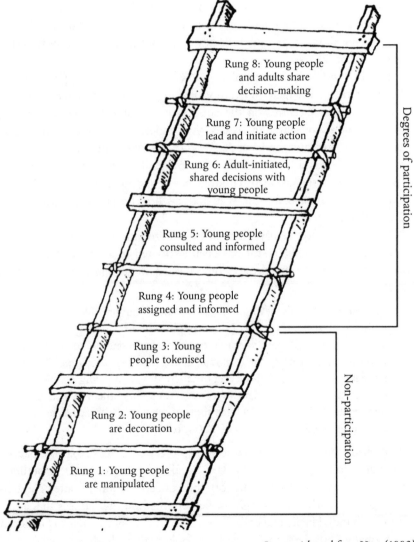

Source: Adapted from Hart (1992)

Figure 2.2 Hart's typology of children's participation

The top rung of the ladder, or the highest level of child participation, is achieved in projects or programmes which are initiated by children, with decision-making shared among children and adults. This is differentiated through various degrees of power-sharing, down to the bottom rung where adults manipulate children, by using them to support causes and pretend that the causes are inspired by children. Hart's analysis of the different models of participatory involvement 'from tokenism to citizenship' suggests that many existing models of participation are decorative, placatory or manipulative, with full power-sharing and involvement by children a rarely achieved goal. We revisit this typology in Chapter 9, where participation in fostering services is considered.

Despite the UK ratification of the UNCRC in 1991, the opportunity for UK children to participate in decision-making can be considered as patchy. Their involvement centres on the concept of children having an evolving capacity to be consulted on issues that concern them (Scarman 1986). Participation literature can be understood to describe children's participation in UK services and communities as haphazard: 'When it comes to the representation or inclusion of children per se in wider decision-making… initiatives have remained local, scattered, ad hoc, fragile and experimental' (Prout 2002, p.x).

The lack of effective participation by children in decision-making about their lives in the public sector has been attributed to a failure to recognise their competencies, as this extract from a discussion of children's participation illustrates:

> frequently children's views are not sought or, if sought, still disregarded within everyday institutions (for example schools), local government settings (for example, social services departments) and national government processes (for example in the drafting of Home Office legislation)… The refusal to accept that children and young people are competent witnesses to their own lives has confined them to a state of impotency, at the mercy of adults, some of whom, as history teaches us, cannot be relied upon. (Hill *et al.* 2004, p.84)

Children's rights, not just to provision and protection, but also to participation, have not been fully enacted in the UK. Legal and policy contexts, as outlined in the introductory chapter, support the concept of looked after children as service users who have a right to be consulted on the services that affect them, both individually and collectively. The process by which foster children are formally consulted, for example at looked after children's social work reviews, might be considered as having been designed in ways that do not give children participation rights, particularly younger children (Thomas 2005).

Children's lack of full participation rights suggests that children are a minority group who lack the power to change their lives (Mayall 1996). Hart's ladder of participation is employed in this study as an analytical device to contextualise children's accounts of their participation in fostering services. Only by participating with adults can they be empowered to use their rights as citizens to transform their lives; if not they are at risk of adult manipulation and retaining a minority position. Effective participation can, however, be considered as an emerging practice within child and family services. The Children Act Guidance and Regulations 2010, implemented on 1 April 2011, places a greater emphasis on children's participation as a way of improving social care practice with looked after children.

The sociology of childhood as a theoretical approach to the study of fostering

A theoretical perspective located in the sociology of childhood offers a useful perspective for the study of fostering. Foundational development approaches were considered earlier in this chapter as being located in a paternalistic paradigm of welfare provision. There are five main supports to my claim that the sociology of childhood offers a contemporary approach to the study of fostering.

First, the sociology of childhood is preferable to foundational development theories, which offer a narrow, deficit model of looked after children, as outlined above.

Second, other areas of social work, such as disability (Oliver 1989), have already moved towards a theory base derived from sociologically informed models. Although the conceptualisation in some of the policy and legal contexts promotes children's participatory rights, the dominant lens through which they are viewed within child and family social work remains a deficit model derived from foundational development theory. The tension between the two models can be considered as parallel to the debate within the disability movement. Understandings of disability previously operated on a deficit, medical model of disability, but have largely been successfully challenged by a social model of disability (Oliver 1989). Whilst the status of other minority groups, notably minority ethnic groups, has also been re-negotiated within emergent theoretical understandings (Thompson 2006), there has not yet been a re-negotiation of the status of children within child and family social work. The status of looked after children is yet to be equated with that of other groups of social work service users.

Third, the sociology of childhood facilitates the contribution of children's own understandings, by fore-grounding children's accounts of their lived experiences. In this way, it is able to facilitate the contribution of children's understandings of being fostered. It is essentially through the contribution of children's accounts that this book attempts to bring a new perspective to the existing knowledge base of fostering.

The fourth support is that a theoretical approach informed by the sociology of childhood might enable an exploration of fostering as positioned in the intermediate or overlap zone between private and public (Nutt 2006). This concept is outlined earlier (see p.41), as its origins lie in the sociology of health (Stacey 1988), although Mayall (2002) has developed this concept within the sociology of childhood. The division between public and private facilitates an exploration of the power dynamics involved in the complex delivery of fostering services and the rights of children who are fostered. The division of the data into private and public facilitates both consideration of children's positions within a foster family and also separately those of their position as recipients of public provision.

Last, the sociology of childhood enables a wider understanding of children's rights, not just those concerned with protection and provision, but also rights to participation. Positioning children as members of society with rights is particularly pertinent for looked after children, since they may lack other sources of advocacy. There is a tension emerging between the use of a deficit model for understanding children's behaviour and the increasing awareness of the participatory rights of looked after children. Understandings that largely attribute poor performance by looked after children to earlier damage from birth parents may serve to maintain the current system. It protects both social workers and foster carers from culpability in the delivery of a service that may fail to meet the needs of children as recipient service users. Shifting to understandings of fostering informed by children themselves could threaten this collusion of adult understandings. The inclusion of children's own understandings as foster children could therefore challenge existing practices in fostering.

The child development model that underpins current research and practice in children and families social work only allows the provision and protection aspects of children's rights to be addressed (Winter 2006). The concept of childhood as a time of protection and opportunity (Mayall 1984) is that of a general understanding of childhood. Looked after children have often experienced their parents' incapacity to protect and nurture them; instead they become children reliant on public provision, in need of both protection and control. In a complex social welfare system where birth parents largely act as advocates for children (Davis and Edwards 2004), understandings of parental advocacy, in navigating welfare or education provisions for children, are not necessarily transferable from the disability arena to that of looked after children. There are additional factors of parental availability to advocate and also the difficulties surrounding the complexity and patchy quality of services for looked after children to be considered. Not all looked after children are members of a birth family; others might only be nominal members.

There is also an acknowledgement that the public provision of welfare fails to provide foster children with a stable and secure family upbringing (Jackson and Thomas 1999; Sinclair 2005). In a review of the research concerning looked after children, Bullock (2006) acknowledges that the task of corporate parenting is a flexible one, with added complexities such as managing relationships with birth relatives. Not all looked after children require parenting by the local authority in the conventional sense. Some are able, or can be enabled, to advocate on their own behalf, where necessary. In this way, a theoretical model which accommodates the positioning of children as people with rights has particular relevance for looked after children.

In summary, the use of a perspective informed by the sociology of childhood may contribute new understandings of fostering in several ways. It locates the knowledge of children who are fostered as central to academic knowledge about fostering, through an understanding of their views and experiences as co-constructors of foster family relationships and as consumers of fostering services. Despite an acknowledgement that children need a voice that is heard and the acceptance in the sociology of childhood of children as competent social actors, many children's professionals continue to rely on the foundational developmental approach to understanding childhood (Wyness 2006). Consideration of fostering as belonging in an intermediate domain (Mayall 1984), or overlap domain (Nutt 2006), have enabled fostering to be explored in an holistic and complex way.

Ambitious policy goals, it is argued by Townsend (1981), can only be achieved by a skilled and qualified workforce whose practice is guided by a professional body of knowledge. To achieve the policy goal of effective participation by children, a body of knowledge is required that can guide social work practice. Developmental psychology is concerned with the private domain of the family, whereas the sociology of childhood enables public, private and intermediate domains to be considered. In essence, the use of a theoretical perspective informed by the sociology of childhood seeks to supplement and update the existent knowledge base of child and family social work. These factors make the sociology of childhood the logical choice for the theoretical approach to a study of fostering.

Chapter summary

This has been a somewhat complicated chapter. In essence it has suggested that understandings from the sociology of childhood, together with concepts such as the intermediate domain (Mayall 1984; Stacey 1988) and the ladder of participation (Hart 1992), offer a holistic framework for the study of fostering, a supplement to the existing theory base of developmentalism.

There is a tension between the positioning of foster children in the legal and policy contexts, as set out in Chapter 1, and their positioning within child and family social work, as set out in this chapter. Beginning with a brief explanation of how understandings from developmental theories dominate child and family social work, we explored four main challenges to that dominance: the lack of acknowledgement of cultural variation in understanding childhoods, that they appraise looked after children on a deficit model, that they fail to acknowledge children as having participatory rights, and finally an acknowledgement that their lack of consideration of children's agency may inhibit broader understandings of childhoods. Next, the sociology of childhood was briefly outlined, followed by two supplementary theoretical concepts, which assist in understanding how fostering operates in both the private arena of family life and in the public arena of welfare services: Stacey's and Mayall's conceptualisation of the intermediate domain, and understandings of child participation.

Five reasons were put forward to support the argument for using an approach drawing on the sociology of childhood for understanding fostering: first, it offers a broader approach; second, it moves child and family social work into a social model of practice; third, it recognises children's lived experiences and opinions; fourth, it acknowledges the complicated public/private positioning of looked after childhoods; and last, it is concerned not just with the provision and protection of children, but also their participation.

The central argument put forward in this chapter is that the use of a broader, sociological approach to fostering updates previous conceptualisations and brings into consideration such areas as children's rights and cultural diversity. In doing so, it aligns fostering with its statutory and policy contexts.

Chapter 3

Fostering Research

As with other areas of social work, knowledge about fostering comes from a variety of sources: practice wisdom, individual retrospective accounts, rhetoric about what ought to happen, and also from research. This chapter aims to explore the evidence base of fostering, looking at the knowledge about fostering which derives from rigorously carried-out research studies conducted in the four countries of the UK since 1997, when New Labour changed much of the UK welfare provision. In the following chapter we explore the research evidence from children's views studies. This chapter, however, is concerned with mainstream, traditional fostering research, beginning with previous overviews of fostering research. We then move on to look at research concerned with foster carers, outcomes achieved by foster children, birth families, placement comparisons, fostering services and kinship care.

Previous overviews of the fostering research literature

Five previous reviews of the fostering literature in the UK from the last decade are critically examined to provide an overview of earlier research in this area. Berridge's major review of fostering research is a starting point (Berridge 1997). An overview by Schofield (Schofield 2003) compared different fostering studies. Two more recent reviews of fostering research literature are explored in order to contextualise current fostering research: first that of Wilson *et al.* in their 2004 scoping review of fostering research for the Social Care Institute of Excellence and, second, Sinclair's review of Department of Health-funded fostering research studies (Sinclair 2005). The final overview is from Sellick, who charts the recent changes in fostering research (Sellick 2006).

Berridge, in *Foster Care: A Research Review* (1997), a national review of fostering research conducted for the Department of Health, scrutinised fostering research in the four countries of the UK over the preceding 20 years. He concluded that, in 1997, fostering was a neglected area of academic research and that most of the existing research had been reliant on secondary or proxy informants, usually social workers, birth parents and foster mothers. Adoption and residential care, by contrast, had attracted more academic interest, although paradoxically the numbers of looked after children in those placements was considerably lower, as noted earlier. Berridge found that only 13 major research studies had focused on fostering. He found few research projects that had actively consulted children and none that had focused exclusively on them. One that had consulted children, a 1995 study by Triseliotis and others in Scotland, reported that half of the 15 teenagers interviewed were satisfied with their fostering placement, although many of the others reported considerable resentment about their placement.

Schofield's *Stability in Foster Care: The Research Overview*, presented to a voluntary fostering support network and published online by the DOH (Schofield 2003), began with the perspective that research on foster care presented many methodological challenges. These were identified as: the difficulty of obtaining a large enough sample, the differing methodologies employed made reviewing the literature complicated, and the interactions between the child, the placement and the services available all varied considerably. One factor identified by her as significant in understanding placement stability, however, was the child or young person's attitude to the placement: when a consistent wish not to be in a particular placement was expressed, there was an increased risk of breakdown.

Foster carers' views concerning the difficulty of their task is a persistent theme in many studies (Ogilvie, Kirton and Beecham 2006; Triseliotis, Borland and Hill 2000). Listening to the views of looked after children was understood by Schofield as an alternative approach to understanding placement stability (Schofield 2003). On key messages for policy and practice, Schofield found general agreement that placement stability would be promoted by: good professional assessments of children's needs and what carers could offer, effective care plans that looked to the long term and also that children were matched to placements and services, with resources matched to both children and foster carers.

In contrast to Berridge's review, Wilson *et al.*, in their 2004 knowledge review for the Social Care Institute for Excellence, explored the research literature in foster care, with a focus on outcomes for children in long-term foster care. The boundaries of their review were of research published since 2000, focusing on empirical studies relevant to fostering in England

and Wales, but including some international studies, largely from the US. Although much data were included *about* children, there was little inclusion of children's perspectives or knowledge. The understandings of foster carers, birth families and social workers were carefully reviewed with an emphasis on identifying best practice in terms of best outcomes for foster children. Wilson *et al.* identified a need for adequate placement choice and planning, with a full range of placements used flexibly after proper assessment and with appropriate support. The efficacy of particular placement choices was largely measured against disruption rates, rather than alternative considerations, such as the child's or birth parents' views.

In scoping the main trends in fostering research, Wilson and colleagues argued that there were two major academic discourses within the literature: one concerned with legislation and policy, the other with the relationships formed within and between fostering and birth families and the social work professionals (Wilson *et al.* 2004). Current classifications of fostering by Wilson and colleagues, adapted from an earlier study by Rowe and colleagues (Rowe, Hundleby and Garnett 1989), distinguished the following types of foster home provision, based on the purposes and length of time for which children are fostered:

Short-term: for emergency, assessment, initial, and remand fostering

Shared-care: regular short breaks, respite care

Medium-term: task-centered, treatment foster care, such as bridging placements or preparation for adoption

Long-term: upbringing.

(Wilson et al. 2004, p.9)

In a major research review, *Fostering Now: Messages from Research*, conducted by Sinclair for the Department of Health in 2005, the findings of 15 research studies were explored, only three of which had included children as participants. As DOH-funded projects, the focus of the studies had resonance with current policy in this area, with an apparent emphasis on outcomes achieved by looked after children and 'measurement' of the difficulties encountered by foster carers in coping with looked after children (Sinclair 2005).

Sellick's recent review of fostering literature was named 'From Famine to Feast', a title that reflects the growth in the knowledge base of fostering since Berridge's own review in this area (Sellick 2006). Drawing on his own extensive research and that of others, in the area of private agency fostering provision, Sellick mapped the changing face of fostering to include the rise of independent fostering agencies and the growth of kinship care. He drew an interesting distinction between fostering as supplementary care, or as substitute care, in relation to the care of birth parents. Attributing the wealth of new fostering research to the New Labour government's policy agenda and investment from 1997, when they came to power, he concluded that Britain would retain a mixed economy of fostering provision.

Despite the methodological difficulties identified by Schofield, these fostering overviews have portrayed a research area that has altered considerably over the last decade, from an under-researched area to one which has become fast moving and rich in complexity, with an emerging acknowledgement that children can and should contribute their own views and experiences to research about fostering. The themes identified from these reviews were the relative absence of children's views, the relative scarcity of research about the way children were placed in foster homes and understandings of fostering as a task to be accomplished and as a time-limited activity.

Foster carers

Triseliotis *et al*.'s study of Scottish foster care, with comparisons to English data (Triseliotis *et al.* 2000), was set up in response to the recruitment crisis within foster care. It aimed to identify the characteristics, motivations and circumstances of existing foster carers and also to examine local authority structures and organisation in respect of fostering. This extensive study, largely undertaken as a self-completion postal questionnaire, included 835 foster carers and former foster carers and senior child-care managers, from all 32 Scottish local authorities and some English ones, plus interviews with social work managers and some 67 foster carers. A six-week census of all foster placements in Scotland was also conducted, in the autumn of 1998. Triseliotis *et al.* (2000) found that respondents in their quantitative survey were frustrated by a social work service that did not seem to share their commitment to children. Foster carers reported that social workers made infrequent visits, were unavailable, unresponsive, lacked warmth, and gave a general feeling that looked after children were a low priority compared to child protection cases. This latter claim can be understood in the context of social services department policies and statutory requirements to prioritise the need to protect children 'at risk', as opposed to the competing demands of children who are 'looked after', and therefore assumed to be safe.

Triseliotis *et al*.'s (2000) foster carers reported 'normal' parenting supports largely from family and neighbourhood networks. Whilst almost all previous studies identify the positive contribution of parental contact to children's well-being and rehabilitation prospects, some foster carers experienced contact as an additional burden, that made an intrusion on their time, privacy and family life. Many of the concerns voiced by foster carers in this extensive study centred not only on the perceived negative impact of parental contact on the child, but also on the disruption, conflict or aggression it caused within the foster home (Triseliotis *et al.* 2000).

Why some carers have more apparent success in offering placement stability to looked after children was explored in an English study of adolescent foster care, conducted in 2002 by Farmer and colleagues. They examined the quality and outcomes for 68 adolescents with 'emotional and behavioural difficulties', from 14 local authorities and two independent fostering agencies. A tripartite research design was used: a review of the young people's individual case files and interviews with young people, their carers and social workers were undertaken at three months and again nine months after placement with a new foster family. Carers who were warm, clear, firm, understanding and not easily put out are identified by Farmer and her colleagues as having lower than expected rates of placement breakdown (Farmer, Moyers and Lipscombe 2004).

A study of remuneration and performance in foster care, by Ogilvie *et al.* (2006), was commissioned by the DOH and conducted in 2001 and 2002. Stage One consisted of a macro-level analysis of remuneration and performance indicators for all local authorities in England. Next, interviews were conducted with foster care managers and focus groups with social workers and foster carers in 15 local authorities and five independent foster care agencies. There was also a postal survey of 1,118 foster carers, which had a return rate of 60 per cent. They found that an emphasis on foster carers' skills and qualifications may overshadow their less measurable but vital personal qualities. If foster carers are to be regarded as part of a skilled social care workforce, then the authors argue that they should also be able to enjoy more of the benefits and rights which would ordinarily accompany employment (Ogilvie *et al.* 2006).

To summarise, the research studies about foster carers illustrate the way in which adult agendas can predominate. These studies recommend the professionalisation of foster carers, although studies of children's views indicate their uneasiness about claims that caring for them is a job, rather than part of 'normal' family life. When children's views were included in studies in this area, new data emerged, such as the characteristics of foster carers being identified as key to placement stability.

Outcomes achieved by fostered children

In 2000 Schofield and colleagues undertook a study of 58 children under the age of ten placed in long-term foster care, from eight local authorities in England. This was concerned with the exploration of how foster carers meet the needs of looked after children, how the nature of the foster parenting might influence outcomes and also the role that social workers and birth parents play in supporting long-term fostering. Using social worker and foster carer questionnaires as a starting point, interviews were conducted with most of the social workers, foster carers and family link workers (elsewhere in the literature referred to as fostering support workers), with 25 birth relatives (of 20 of the children) and with 37 of the foster children, with an age range of 4–12 years (Schofield *et al.* 2000).

Schofield appraised the quality of success of the placements in terms of attachment theory, with early assessment made of the foster children's attachment status and the quality of care received from the birth relatives. Previous foster placements were identified: 13 children had had only one foster placement, 20 had had two, eight had had three, ten had had four and seven of the children had had five or more placements. Reports of the first stage of that study (Schofield *et al.* 2000) found that fostering was under-resourced: there was an urgent need for expert social work, and a lack of both prescribed models of good practice and appropriate educational and therapeutic support. Schofield also studied children's and young people's perspectives on fostering and identified the following three findings. First, children and young people wanted greater consultation about moves of placement, education, contact, change of social worker and more information about foster carers. Second, children and young people wanted their individuality to be respected and for stereotypes of looked after children to be avoided. Last, many children and young people expressed positive views of foster care, particularly in offering stability and supporting education and ambition.

Research concerning outcomes is largely conducted by longitudinal studies, with a major study by Sinclair, Baker, Wilson and Gibbs conducted between 1998 and 2001 in three stages, which contributed both quantitative and qualitative data (Sinclair *et al.* 2005). In the first stage of this study, a postal survey of 495 foster carers, 416 social workers, 492 link (fostering specialist social workers) workers and 150 foster children, aged from 5 to 18 years and older, was conducted. Twenty-four case studies were also undertaken. Stage Two consisted of a broadly similar research design, but achieved a smaller sample of social workers (337).

Stage Three of Sinclair *et al.*'s study, in 2001, included a larger data collection process, with birth parents, adoptive parents and 231 foster children, plus 116 former foster children from the earlier stages of the study who were now living independently and 22 now in residential care. Thirty case studies were additionally conducted in Stage Three; 87 interviews were undertaken with participants from the postal surveys. Of those, 15 were with foster children and five with other young people (age not specified other than 5–18 years and over). As noted, the focus was on outcomes. Three groups stood out: those 'whose placements were going well', those 'apparently not going well' and an 'intermediate' group. The analysis, of the statistical, qualitative and case study data, sought similar explanations from the different datasets. Children themselves reported feeling safer in foster care and considered that they did better than they would have done at home. Few children, however, stayed in the same foster home and viewed it as a 'permanent base'.

Sinclair *et al.* suggest that foster care can often be considered 'impressive, when viewed as an isolated experience' (Sinclair *et al.* 2005, p.264), in offering looked after children a good, short-term experience of family life. If viewed as part of a 'care career', it too often offers a truncated, tantalising and disrupted experience of family life, followed by stressful and ill-supported moves, either back to the birth family, residential care or to independent living (Sinclair *et al.* 2005, p.264). This situation was largely attributed by Sinclair *et al.* to the lack of social services resources, poor job prospects for care-leavers and the ambivalent relationships that many foster children have with their birth parents (Sinclair *et al.* 2005). It is notable that the younger foster children, aged under ten years, in Schofield's (2000) study reported that they appreciated the stability of their foster placement. However, the findings from Sinclair *et al.*'s study have similarity to those from a research review about stability by Jackson and Thomas (1999) which found that placement instability affected half of children entering care, and most teenagers. In contrast, Schofield's (2003) qualitative study of long-term foster care explored the durability of fostering relationships. Through interviews with 40 English young adults who had been previously fostered, she found that in adult life many former foster children still saw themselves as part of their foster family (Schofield 2003).

Broad's longitudinal study of the outcomes achieved by children and young people fostered in one voluntary fostering agency recently reported the findings from Stage One of the study (Broad 2008). Fifty-three children and young people who were fostered and 56 carers participated in this postal survey. That makes this a study that integrated children's and adults' views. The survey was piloted with foster children from the same agency, then amended to accommodate the children's requests for more colour and tick-box answers. Of the 24 girls and 32 boys who took part, the majority were white English, with four reporting their ethnicity as 'Asian' and three as 'mixed black'. All had been fostered by the same carers for at least six months at the time of the survey. The questions from the survey enquired about areas such as how much say children felt they had about placements and reviews, how children thought they were achieving educationally and in the acquisition of life skills, their connections with family and friends and their activities.

The findings indicated a high level of involvement in decision-making inside the home, but less in key decisions about their lives or arrangements for reviews (Broad 2008). They reported wanting to be treated as 'normal' at home, school and by the authorities. Although they mostly reported that their current foster carer was the most important person in their life, most children still wanted more contact with their own family. Children's reports about school were mixed: they largely thought that they contributed, felt safe and had people to whom they could talk, but attainment, behaviour and making friends were difficult for some children. In terms of life skills, children considered hygiene, talking with others and using a computer to be their strengths. Doing laundry, travelling independently, budgeting and using local services were skills rated as needing support. Some gender differences were apparent in the life skills responses: boys, for example, rated their computer skills well, but their domestic skills were lower (Broad 2008).

Carers were asked about three distinct areas: their support needs, their views about their foster child's health and well-being and any changes they had detected in their foster child since the beginning of the placement. The findings for these voluntary agency foster carers were generally more favourable than for other studies of foster carers: most carers reported agency social work support as good or excellent, although this specialist social work agency did not have to balance the competing needs of child protection responsibilities. There was a reported gradual improvement in reports of children's achievements, although the biggest difficulty was children's behaviour, which 24 of the carers reported as a challenge at the beginning with little improvement over time. The greatest reported improvements were in the areas of self-care, health and relationships, but educational achievement had remained static throughout the placement. Comparisons between the reported understandings of children and carers in Broad's study are problematic, since they were asked about different aspects of fostering. A study by Farmer and colleagues (2007), which also used a postal survey of carers and children looked after through a voluntary agency, as part of the data collected to consider children's progress and outcomes, reached similar findings.

As these studies illustrate, younger children in foster care have greater stability and achieve better outcomes than older looked after children, but many report satisfaction with their foster family, if not with their involvement in decision-making about their lives.

Birth family

Despite acknowledgement in the policy and legal frameworks of the role of birth parents as stakeholders in fostering, research studies based upon birth parents' views or accounts are sparse. Sinclair's outcome-focused study, which was examined above, identified foster children's relationships with their birth parents as one of the variables in placement stability, with an unresolved ambivalent parental relationship found to be detrimental to establishing permanence in fostering placements. Most recent studies in this area, however, focus on contact between foster children and their birth parents, with earlier assumptions that contact promoted good outcomes for foster children now challenged by research findings such as Sinclair's. This study portrayed a more complex relationship, with ongoing concerns noted by foster carers and social workers that, within some birth families, there remained ongoing risks of physical abuse, neglect and emotional abuse from some members of the birth family household, despite the foster child having moved to live with a foster family (Sinclair *et al.* 2005). Beneficial contact with a family member was, however, identified in the 2002 study by Farmer *et al.* as being linked to better outcomes for foster children in a number of ways (Farmer *et al.* 2004).

Cleaver's (2000) study of foster children's contact was undertaken for the DOH. In a retrospective survey of 152 social work files, with an accompanying qualitative study of interviews with 33 foster children and their parents, carers and social workers, Cleaver identified four main venues for contact: the home of the birth parent or parents, the foster home, social services premises or a public leisure facility. She interviewed children aged 5–12 years old twice, once six weeks after placement and again 12 months later. The birth parent's/s' home was identified by both children and their families as the most popular meeting place (Cleaver 2000).

In summary, the little research that exists about foster children's contact with their birth families indicates that the more recent research study challenged previous understandings that this contact is generally beneficial for children. For many looked after children and young people, however, their birth relatives may offer the only permanent relationships that endure throughout their childhood.

Comparisons between fostering and other types of care

Adoption is predominant as the placement of choice in current social policy for children who are unlikely to be rehabilitated to their birth family, as noted earlier. This has resonance with policy aims of creating permanence for looked after children and the current preoccupation in the fostering research literature for evaluating the effectiveness of long-term fostering.

Sellick and Thoburn (1996) provided an early summary of the research on foster placement breakdown rates. Citing Rowe *et al.* (1989), Berridge and Cleaver (1987) and Kelly (1995), they concluded that there is consistency in breakdown rates both across the respective studies and also between adoption and fostering placements. Breakdown rates are reportedly highest for children in middle childhood, with the 46 per cent rate reported by Berridge and Cleaver being consistent with other studies.

Quinton and colleagues (1998) undertook a qualitative, multi-method small-scale study of 61 children aged from five to nine years who were placed either for adoption or fostering. This study relied on psychological assessments of children's difficulties, and extensive interviewing of the adult stakeholders, but not the children themselves (Quinton *et al.* 1998). The children are categorised by the degree of disturbance exhibited in their emotional and behavioural development and the findings are concerned with the comparative breakdown rates of adopted and fostered children. In this study the cause of the placement breakdown is largely attributed to understandings derived from attachment theories, in that children's experiences of earlier poor parenting were considered to have precluded their healthy attachment to substitute carers.

Eleven per cent of looked after children are placed in residential care (DCSF 2008). The main studies comparing residential and foster care are somewhat dated, and therefore fall outside the timeframe of this review. Nevertheless they contribute to understandings of the increased popularity of fostering and so are briefly mentioned. It was argued that residential and foster care were complementary provisions (Wagner 1998), and that residential care was more appropriate for some children. A key study that compared residential and foster care was conducted in 1988, by Colton and colleagues (Colton, Sanders and Williams 1988). The main findings, however, remain significant. Forty per cent of children entering residential care with a 'clean' criminal record acquired either a police caution or a conviction within six months. A high number of children, also 40 per cent, reported being bullied or harassed, with many reporting suicidal feelings.

These comparisons give the impression of fostering as the appropriate provision for the majority of looked after children; however, the youngest children with weak birth family ties and few behavioural 'difficulties' are considered for adoption. Older children and those with challenging behavioural 'difficulties' are more likely to be considered for residential care.

Fostering services

The organisation and delivery of fostering services by 94 local authorities in England were studied by Waterhouse in 1997, using a postal survey. She found that only 20 per cent of local authorities were able to offer a choice of foster home to social workers seeking fostering placements for looked after children under ten years old. This fell to 3 per cent for children aged ten or over (Waterhouse 1997). There were also insufficient numbers of foster carers, with better status for foster carers seen as a way to redress this. These findings illustrate the lack of resources to appropriately match looked after children and young people to a foster family, with the overwhelming number of fostering placements made as a matter of expediency.

There is little evidence that either foster carers or foster children are involved in the design, delivery or monitoring of fostering services within their agencies. For example, Thomas and O'Kane, in a 1998 survey of 225 children who were looked after by seven local authorities, undertook a detailed study of 45 of those children using interviews, participatory techniques and group discussion, to learn more about their perspectives on the decision-making processes for looked after children (Thomas and O'Kane 1998). They identified factors that assisted or impeded children's involvement in decision-making.

Triseliotis et al. (2000) also found that foster carers were not involved in the design, delivery and monitoring of fostering services, with the exception of recruitment and training, and participation on management panels. As Triseliotis et al. found, 'the regular involvement of carers in the authorities fostering activities in both Scotland and England was infrequent' (Triseliotis et al. 2000, p.100). This has resonance with understandings of children's participation within children's services as fragmented and patchy (Hill et al. 2004; Prout 2002; Thomas and O'Kane 1998).

Morgan's (2005) study of foster care in England sought the views of foster children, foster carers and birth parents. Local authorities and fostering agencies contacted the participants: 410 foster children, 303 foster carers and 20 birth parents all completed postal questionnaires. The study found that children considered that having information about a family before they moved was important: ethnicity, religion and whether or not there were children in the family were the most important things children wanted to know about. Two-thirds of children had not had any part in the choice of their placement. Most foster children appreciated the opportunities available to them, particularly having a family who looked after them well; they did better at school and became independent. The worst aspects were missing birth relatives and friends and feeling 'like the odd one out' (Morgan 2005, p.17). Although 75 per cent of foster children said that their views were considered in the foster home, the same number said that their views were not considered in care planning. The private domain of the foster family proved more responsive to their participation in decision-making than the public domain that had a statutory responsibility to consider foster children's views.

The process of organising fostering is therefore largely determined by local authorities and children's trusts, with guidance from central government. It is here understood as a process that has little input from foster carers, fostered children or birth families.

Kinship fostering

Rates of formal kinship care have increased from the 3 per cent of foster carers identified by Rowe as children's relatives (Rowe *et al.* 1989), to the 18 per cent identified by Richards and Tapsfield in 2003 (Richards and Tapsfield 2003). There is some discrepancy in the literature over whether or not kinship care is considered as foster care, with Triseliotis *et al.* (2000) reporting an average of 10 per cent of foster care as care from relations. Some local authorities pay kinship carers lower fostering rates: some do not vet them as foster carers because of financial concerns, or concerns that they might not meet the more stringent requirements of foster parent vetting. This makes kinship care a complex area to define and therefore to quantify (Triseliotis *et al.* 2000). The most recent government statistics (DCSF 2010) report that 11 per cent of looked after children are fostered by birth relatives.

A study by Farmer and Moyers (2005) for the DfES concerning the placement pattern and outcomes of children and young people placed with relatives or friends differentiated between 'stranger foster care' and 'kinship foster care'. Farmer and Moyers found that those children fostered by relatives tended to achieve marginally better stability rates, despite kinship carers' generally less favourable circumstances in terms of age, health, levels of single parenting and housing provision.

Studies by Broad and colleagues of kinship carers in a London borough examined a total of 120 kinship care placements, over a three-year period. The first study explored the status of kinship care placements for 70 children (who were between 1 and 16 years of age). The second study, funded by the Joseph Rowntree Foundation, examined 50 kinship care placements of children and young people aged 11–25 (Broad, Hayes and Rushforth 2001). 'Descriptive statistical data' were collected on the 50 young people. Individual interviews were done with 22 young people, 13 kinship carers and 25 social workers. Overall they found a higher proportion of black and minority ethnic children in kinship care than in local authority care, with a better match of children to kinship carers from the same racial and cultural background. Broad and colleagues argued that there remain many unanswered questions about public and private roles, rights and responsibilities in the concept of kinship care. The key question that they identified was to establish the role of the state, if any, in organising, supporting and endorsing kinship care arrangements.

Overall, studies of kinship care demonstrate that better outcomes are achieved by children and young people who are looked after by carers from within their own family and social networks. This factor, together with the lower resource implications for social services departments, can explain the growing popularity of kinship care as a placement of choice.

Chapter summary

We've now looked at some of the key overviews and research studies concerned with foster carers, outcomes achieved by foster children, birth families, placement comparisons, fostering services and kinship care. This has given us a sound grasp of the evidence base of fostering that is derived from research data. Issues of concern identified in the UK fostering literature centre largely around the following four areas: first, that there is an inadequate supply of foster carers; second, that the current foster caring task itself is ambiguous, for example temporary carers are largely undertaking full parenting responsibilities (Berridge and Cleaver 1987); third, that some of the children requiring fostering are 'very troubled and troublesome' (Triseliotis et al. 2000, p.2); and last, that children and young people from care achieve poor outcomes (Sinclair et al. 2005).

Three themes ran through much of the fostering research literature. The first is that fostering studies that fail to take children's views into account can produce findings that are at odds with those from studies of children's views, as we shall go on to explore in the next chapter. One example of these differing standpoints is that from the children's views studies there is an expectation that fostering should be 'normalised', that looked after children should be treated the same as any other children. In contrast, the traditional evidence base of fostering frequently recommends that fostering should be increasingly 'professionalised'. This different standpoint will become more apparent in the following chapter about children's views studies. A second theme is a general lack of debate about key concerns in fostering, with a clear consensus about issues such as the lack of sufficient numbers of carers from which to match individual children and the increasingly complex difficulties presented by looked after children and young people. Third, there is also an apparent disjuncture between social policy and social work practice in fostering: what is supposed to happen and what actually happens to looked after children as they progress through the care system? Upholding children's rights and caring for children successfully so that they achieve good outcomes is not apparent from the research findings explored in this chapter.

Chapter 4

What Children and Young People Say about Being Fostered

There are many reasons why caring professionals need to take on board the key messages from children's views studies. The most important of these are that children and young people who are fostered are the key witnesses to their complicated and idiosyncratic lives and experiences. As a group, they are vulnerable, under-achieving, often isolated and usually lacking in stability and security. To plan for children and young people in ways which enable them to achieve better outcomes, we need to understand from their firsthand accounts what is really happening to them.

Children's views about their services have been gathered carefully over the last 30 years; but these have then been largely ignored in terms of the delivery of services to the children. The studies considered here are, first, those studies undertaken before 1998, when the welfare policy changed with the incoming New Labour government. Their new welfare agenda was first outlined in the white paper *Modernising Social Services* (DOH 1998). Children's rights, child participation and the evaluation of services through the measurement of outcomes became an integral part of social policy for looked after children and young people. This chapter sets out the main children's views studies about how fostering and social work with children and young people who are fostered might be improved. Children's views about their social workers, their understandings of and participation in the care system and their views about support and advocacy services are all separately considered. The final section draws together the key messages from these studies and considers the implications of re-positioning children's rights within the arena of fostering.

Early studies of children's views of fostering

Thorpe's (1980) research study was concerned with 121 children and young people, aged 5–17 years, who had been in their foster placement for at least a year (Thorpe 1980). It was conducted in England in 1971–1972, in a Midland local authority. The wider study drew on interview data from the children and young people themselves, their carers and also their social workers. All the children and young people were interviewed about what they thought and felt about being in care. Findings included three themes: of children's feelings of 'not belonging', 'needing a proper home' and insecurities about 'being sent back'. Thorpe concluded that children needed to know what was going to happen to them and that greater attention to planning about their care was required, with children and young people needing to be involved in that planning.

Rowe and colleagues undertook a study of foster children whose carers had applied to adopt them, after a minimum of three years as a foster child in that family (Rowe et al. 1984). The study took place – between 1976 and 1978 – in 21 English local authorities. As part of the wider study, 139 children and young people aged 7–19 years old were interviewed, 39 of whom were in kinship placements. The majority of the sample was white British, four children were black Caribbean and 21 described as 'mixed'. In comparison to the data from other sources – social work records and interviews with social workers and foster carers – Rowe's analysis of the data from children highlighted the gap between the ideal of fostering and the reality. Most of the time, and particularly when things were going well, children did not think much about their status as fostered children. Most were positive about their foster homes and appreciated their carers. Many were anxious about their status, for example 54 per cent had concerns about not being fully integrated into the family where they were fostered and some felt insecure, with concerns that they might be 'taken away'.

Although most understood what fostering was, only 15 of the children in Rowe's study understood the role of social services. This lack of knowledge added to children's insecurity about what might happen if their foster carers were no longer able to keep them. Name differences, having to explain their status to peers and being ethnically different from other foster family members were all problematic for some children. Most children were curious about their birth parents and wanted to know what they looked like, but only 20 per cent had a photograph of them. Overall, Rowe et al. concluded that most were positive about their foster family, but a 'disturbingly large minority' were coping with fears and doubts (Rowe et al. 1984, p.138).

By the mid-1990s, there were several research studies that included children's views. One such was Triseliotis et al.'s (1995) research study, carried out in five local authorities in England and Scotland, to explore social services' responses to teenagers on supervision orders or those looked after in care. The aim was to examine the relationship between children's needs, the social work intervention and the outcomes achieved over a three-year period. Some data gathered were about young people's perceptions of their social work service. One hundred and five young people were interviewed, most on two occasions at least a year apart. Only 15 young people were in foster care.

Most of those said they got on well with their foster carers at the first interview. Being trusted and treated like the carers' own children were particularly valued. At the second interview, ten of the young people thought that they had been helped to deal with the problems that had caused their admission into care. Some appreciated being supported educationally or helped to improve their behaviour. Ten young people identified some difficulties in the placement; five said there was nothing good about the placement and some of this group had experienced profound difficulties: two had been sexually abused by their carers. Rules such as 'coming-in times', and disputes about rules, were the main source of discontent. Even those who had experienced difficulties did not reject fostering per se, but thought, for example, that more flexible carers nearer to the young person's home would be preferable. Triseliotis *et al.* concluded that the key factors for placement success were, first, young people's feelings of being cared for and respected and, second, that there was agreement between foster carers and the young person about their level of autonomy (Triseliotis *et al.* 1995, p.192).

Buchanan's study of 45 looked after children sought their views on children's changed status arising from the Children Act 1989 (Buchanan 1995). She encountered difficulties in finding a representative sample of children and young people, an obstacle that persists in many current studies. The sample, aged 12–17, were both in residential placements and foster care, with those fostered in the minority. There were more girls than boys. Six discussion groups considered topics such as 'choices', 'carers' and 'planning meetings and reviews'. Similar discussions also took place with three groups of carers.

Buchanan found that young people knew little about their rights; they wanted to be better informed. For example, most did not know that they could refuse to have an annual medical examination. There was also evidence that, although young people had been consulted about future planning for them, this was often largely tokenistic with few real choices available. The stigma of being in care, differences of opinion with social workers about contact, bullying, self-harm, disputes about allowances and educational disruptions caused by moving placements were all of concern to this group of looked after children. Some of these findings, for example being bullied by other looked after children, were thought to be related to residential provision, but other themes were considered to have relevance for those in both placement types. The reports from young people that review meetings were intimidating appears to persist across both groups. Buchanan concluded that 'young people have important and highly relevant things to say about the services they are receiving' (Buchanan 1995, p.693).

A long-term study in Northern Ireland of long-term foster care included children's perspectives (McAuley 1996). Nineteen children aged between 4 and 11 years were interviewed 4 months, 12 months and 24 months after placement with long-term 'stranger' foster carers. All the children were interviewed by McAuley at her university, within 'child-friendly' accommodation, using semi-structured interviews with a variety of 'direct work' methods. One such method was 'feeling faces', where children select one from a variety of drawings of faces, in order to indicate their feelings.

There were four main findings. First, that children had experienced the loss of friends, school and significant others by moving to their current placement. They largely reported feeling sad, lonely, angry or afraid about the move. Second, children remained preoccupied with their birth families, whether or not they had continuing contact with them. Third, children were concerned about whether or not their parents had given permission for them to be fostered: those children with a parent opposed to the move were troubled by this. Fourth, children largely chose to keep their preoccupations and feelings about their birth parents private, data which only arose from the indirect research methods such as drawing games, not during the interviews. Standardised psychometric testing for family intimacy rated these foster children at a low level of family intimacy. This meant, for example, that, although most of the sample would share current concerns with their foster mother, they did not share confidences about their past experiences. This latter finding has ongoing implications for social work and fostering practice.

Kosonen undertook a qualitative study of foster children's sibling relationships in one Scottish local authority (Kosonen 1998). Twenty-one children, aged 8–12 years, from 11 families were interviewed and also completed a standardised questionnaire about family relationships. Some were placed with their siblings; others had siblings in different placements, or siblings who remained with birth parents. Some children reported positive relationships with their siblings, which were often related to shared experiences of adversity and resilience. Typically this group had not been separated from their siblings and most had at least one supportive sibling, who helped with tasks, resources or support. Most children missed their siblings and worried about them when they were living apart. Most could identify both positive and negative aspects of their sibling relationships, although some children were considered by Kosonen to be emotionally detached from their siblings, with whom they lived parallel, rather than shared, lives. These siblings had usually experienced long separations from each other. For six children, their siblings were seen as negative, with relationships marred by bullying and rejection. Overall, foster children's relationships were found to be complex and highly individualised, with some suggestion that sibling relationships were more extreme for children who were fostered than for those in the general population.

All six of these early studies sought children's perspectives of being fostered. Some explored atypical groups of foster children, such as young offenders (Triseliotis *et al.* 1995) or those being adopted by their carers (Rowe *et al.* 1984). Other studies focused on particular aspects of being fostered, such as relationships with birth siblings (Kosonen 1998) or the (then) newly acquired rights afforded by the Children Act 1989 (Buchanan 1995). One thread that runs through all these studies is the way children and young people who were fostered largely expressed ignorance about their own histories and their rights as looked after children. Most expressed a wish to be better informed. Many remembered and were troubled by earlier adversities and losses, some of which were attributed to care from birth parents but some were due to changes of neighbourhood, school or placement. These adversities were usually kept private. These early studies illustrate the way in which most foster children reported feeling largely happy with their foster home, despite some insecurities and concerns. There are, however, a significant minority who were not happy: this group are vulnerable, isolated and troubled, with little awareness of their rights.

Voluntary agencies concerned with vulnerable children championed much of the early British research based on children's own accounts of their experiences: ChildLine (Morris and Wheatley 1994), NCH Action for Children (Abrahams 1997), the National Society for the Prevention of Cruelty to Children (NSPCC) (Butler and Williamson 1994) and the Who Cares? Trust (Shaw 1998). Since that time there has been an increased general interest in children's views, including those statutory agencies keen to discharge their statutory responsibilities to consult children on the services that have an impact on their lives. Children's participation has become a fast-moving area of research, as well as a theoretical concept and a policy goal. There has now been a great deal of work that incorporates children's views. Many of these studies have drawn on understandings from the sociology of childhood, in particular understandings that children are the experts about their lived experiences.

Children's views about social workers

Several studies have been undertaken that sought children and young people's opinions about social workers. The earliest of these was Butler and

Williamson's (1994) study *Children Speak: Children, Trauma and Social Work*, which was commissioned by the NSPCC. This was the first study to establish children and young people's understandings about their lived experiences of receiving social work support.

In response to questions about to whom children might talk about their problems (Butler and Williamson 1994), the majority reported that they would talk first to someone within their family network. Many young people reported that they had no trust in other people. Over a quarter said that they would talk to a friend, but a significant number had no trust in adult professionals. Young people's views about social workers centred on social workers' perceived lack of respect for children's confidentiality and their lack of responsiveness to children's concerns, as these quotes from the research report explain:

Social workers don't listen.

They think they make the best decisions for you when they don't even know you.

They always tell someone else – you might not want them to.

(Butler and Williamson 1994, p.94)

The third area of findings established what children wanted from professionals. This was someone who was a good listener, who was available, non-judgemental and non-directive, who maintained children's confidentiality, who had a sense of humour, who was straight talking and who was someone whom children could trust. Children and young people wanted absolute confidentiality. This was understood by Butler and Williamson to mean that, even when social workers wanted to seek advice about children's problems, they should either do this with the child's permission or anonymously (Butler and Williamson 1994, p.91). Not all social workers were viewed negatively, as one 15-year-old girl from the study explains in talking about what was good about her social worker:

She's nice, she understands me. She listens to me, I trust her. She tries to sort out my problems. She's funny, she makes me laugh. I'd advise her for anyone. I'm pleased with the support I've had – she's been someone I can turn to.

(Butler and Williamson 1994, p.95)

Thomas and O'Kane's (1998) *Children and Decision Making* study considered three aspects of children's participation in the looked after children's system, one aspect of which was how they worked with social services, in particular social workers. The findings were similar to those of Butler and Williamson (1994): Thomas and O'Kane found that children and young people in their study reported that their ideal social worker had good communication and listening skills, was understanding, helpful, caring, trustworthy and fair, had a positive personal style, was willing to advocate for children and would sometimes take them out. Concerns about social workers included that they visited at their own convenience or by arrangement with carers, meaning that children were not told when they were coming. They also needed to be more accessible to children by phone. In response to the question 'What makes a good social worker?', children in Thomas and O'Kane's study said:

> They don't make decisions for you; they listen to you – really, isn't it?
>
> They don't butt in on what you say.
>
> It is someone you can talk to.
>
> Someone who helps you sort out your problems.
>
> *(Thomas and O'Kane 1998, p.23)*

Morgan's (2006a) study also found that overall children and young people regarded social workers positively. They wanted social workers to be easier to reach, to follow through on their promises and to see children and young people alone during visits (Morgan 2006a).

Although this chapter is primarily concerned with studies from the four countries of the UK, the following Danish study, into foster children's participation in children's services, by Warming (2006), has been included as it illustrates the frustration experienced by young people who are fostered about their relationships with social workers. Warming undertook interviews with foster children and also set up an interactive discussion board (chat-room) for looked after children and young people, where they could talk to each other. The following quote from the discussion board is from Adda, a 19-year-old former foster child:

> You can't trust the municipality [local authority] at all. They write down everything that you say, and they twist it, so it fits into their fucked up ideas… One doesn't really have any adults that one can trust and from whom one can seek help, because everyone has to report to those higher in the system!!! And the adults always think that what you do and say is because of the problems you faced as a baby.
>
> *(Warming 2006, p.3)*

Warming's findings articulate the way in which children and young people understand their relationships with social workers. Children reported that they thought that social workers attributed their current difficulties to a problematic infancy, as the account above explains. For trust to develop, Warming suggested that social workers would need to move from their position of power to involve, understand and listen to children. She found, however, that social workers typically categorised children by types of problems and 'blamed' them for their problems and behaviour, which are 'diagnosed' with reference to the care children received in infancy. It therefore became problematic for children to develop trust in their social workers. Theorising from these findings, Warming considered that looked after children were in a position of double oppression: first, due to their position in the generational order, as a child relating to an adult social worker, and second, due to their position as a client in relation to the professional social worker (Warming 2006).

As part of a project undertaken by the author and colleagues (Goodyer and Higgins 2010) for the purpose of updating the qualifying social work curriculum at a London university, we consulted a care-leavers group. Overall, the participants had clear ideas about what makes for good and bad social workers. In general, the young people wanted social work students to be taught more social work skills. They were also clear in their expectations that qualifying social workers should work in a way that prioritised their commitment to working with and for young people. The key messages for qualifying social workers were the following:

- They should be really caring and not just doing their job and being officious, for example they should send the child or young person a birthday card.

- They should act for children, *not* managers. They shouldn't always take 'no' for an answer but be willing to challenge social work managers to make them more responsive to children and young people's needs.

- They should offer an individual service, not pro forma letters.

- They should be able to explain things properly and respect children and young people's privacy, especially when breaching privacy causes comeback for the children if, for example, they had complained about parents or carers.

- They should get to know children and young people – their strengths as well as the problems. They should also stay around and not work for an agency.

The studies in this section suggest that children distinguish between social workers as 'good' or 'bad'. There is a consistency in the ways that 'good' social workers were reported: largely they are available, responsive, listen to and advocate for children and can be trusted to do so. 'Bad' social workers, however, failed tests of confidentiality, trust and availability.

Children's understandings of the care system

The opinions of looked after children about their situations are not widely reported in the research and practice literature, but a notable exception was Schofield *et al.* (2000), who interviewed 58 looked after children, from eight different local authorities in England. They found that children reported positive aspects of being looked after, such as having better practical care and protection. They balanced this against the loss of their previous relationships and the stigma surrounding their new situation. Despite the change in terminology from 'being in care' to being 'looked after' which was heralded with the 1989 Children Act, the social stigma surrounding being 'in care' persists. Schofield *et al.* suggested that this stigma was exacerbated by the news media, with public attention focused on factors such as care-leavers having low rates of employment. The low status socially attributed to being 'in care' for many looked after children replaced the stigma surrounding the reasons for their admission to the care system, often associated with general neglect and preoccupied parents. One eight-year-old looked after girl reported that earlier playground taunts of 'being smelly' and having 'no friends' were replaced by taunts of 'At least my mum and dad didn't get rid of me' (Schofield *et al.* 2000). Schofield *et al.*'s study identified two sources of stigma for looked after children: parental failure and care status (Schofield *et al.* 2000).

Brannen *et al.*'s comparative study (Brannen, Heptinstall and Bhopal 2000) looked at children's understandings of care and their views on family life, and was carried out in multi-ethnic areas of London. Sixty-three children were interviewed. They were selected randomly from a survey which included 1,000 children and also from social services' nominations, in four differing family types: step-families, single-parent families, two-parent families and foster families. Fifteen foster children aged 10–13 were interviewed. This study is discussed here at some length, because of the unique insights to some of the characteristics of foster children as a distinct social category.

The authors perceived that, in comparison to children living in step-families, single-parent families or two-parent families, the foster children had the most unpromising circumstances, having experienced the fragmentation of their birth families and moves away from kinship, neighbourhood and social networks. The research findings described foster children as having some views in common with the other groups of children, but some unique understandings and views. Some evidence supported the view that foster children tended to have more idealised concepts of 'proper families' than other groups of children. Having had more disrupted family lives, they reported ambivalence towards absent parents, but with a symbolic attachment to absent siblings. Foster children, and also the other groups of children in this study, see parenting as giving love and care.

In Brannen *et al.*'s (2000) study, children reported that both foster carers and step-parents had to earn their importance in children's lives, through care and support. In the absence of children's own explanations, Brannen *et al.* attributed foster children's ambivalence about absent birth parents to feelings of love, anger, disappointment and betrayal. However, for all the children in the study, birth parents were important, whatever the qualities of the relationships or the particular circumstances.

In most family types, rules were reported in four areas of family life: with respect to personal hygiene, personal behaviour, risk and safety, and helping in the home. Interestingly, one of the main perceived differences in family life, across the four family types, concerned rules for helping in the home. Children, as adults, liked to portray themselves as morally deserving at interview: in this context all four groups of children saw themselves as obedient to the household rules. Although the tasks foster children reported were similar to those of other groups, the foster children expressed wariness about being exploited by adults. This was confirmed, in part, by the interviews when foster carers reported that they were directive about rules and in their parenting style, justifying their rules on the grounds that foster children needed to be clear as to the expected norms in their foster families, especially since they considered that foster children had lacked clear boundaries in their families of origin (Brannen *et al.* 2000).

Other notable differences across the four groups of children lay in social and family networks, with foster children reporting contact with fewer grandparents (typically only one grandparent) and fewer friends than other groups of children. The friendships of foster children showed pronounced characteristics, which the authors attributed to the life changes that children had experienced. Some foster children, but none from the other groups, reported that people who provide public services were significant for them, for example social workers. Although children gave accounts of either being currently settled or not in their foster homes, their carers gave accounts of long and painful periods of adjustment. Carers reported that they shielded the foster children from adult problems, far more than the other categories of parents (Brannen *et al.* 2000).

Children who lived with a foster family showed some marked differences from other groups of children (Brannen *et al.* 2000): in general they seemed to have less intimate parental relations with foster carers, who for example shielded them from adult problems. They had also experienced the fragmentation of their birth families and moves away from kinship, neighbourhood and social networks.

Barnardo's (2008) survey of 66 young people aged between 16 and 21 years who had been in care focused on their school life and education, exploring the factors that had influenced their educational progress. In comparing the experiences of children in local authority care, to those of 'non-looked after children', Barnardo's commissioned a national opinion poll seeking the views of 500 parents or carers of Year 11 pupils, aged 15–16 years. The survey asked questions about placements, schools, exclusions, support received and qualifications gained.

Some of the main differences between the two groups were about looked after children being bullied, having many more home and school moves and a lack of encouragement and support. Most of the care-leavers group reported that they had attended five schools. Almost half the group had attended more than six schools and seven of them had attended more than ten different schools. Over half the young people in the care-leavers group also reported that they had been bullied at school. They believed that this was directly related to their care status, compared to 28 per cent of the non-looked after children who had reportedly been bullied at school. Two-thirds of the care-leavers group reported that they had been treated differently in school because they were in care. Some considered that they were stereotyped as being troublesome while others said that they had been helped, for example by allowances made for disruptions in their life. Not all the young people who had been treated differently had welcomed being singled out rather than being allowed to be 'just one of the class'. In comparison to the non-looked after group, the care-leavers group had received an education that was relatively marked by disruption, a lack of support and stigma.

A nationwide consultation with children and young people who are looked after was carried out as part of the Blueprint Project (VCC 2003) jointly by two voluntary agencies: the Voice of the Child in Care (VCC) and the National Children's Bureau (NCB). The project aimed to map the current care system and to come up with a plan for how it could be improved. Children and young people were consulted as part of this study.

Young people reported that they wanted to be involved in decision-making in their own way; for example, they wanted to choose who came to their reviews, where and when the reviews were held, that people turned up on time and that the meeting did not last too long. Young people did not just want to be involved; they wanted to gain some control and to be involved in discussions about what decisions were going to be made. The need for some control can be understood in a context that acknowledges the realities of looked after childhoods, as illustrated by the following comments from a young person and a social work manager:

> People keep on coming and going. When you're in the care system that's just what life is. (Young person)

I think that the system can work against children achieving a sense of membership in their foster families. A lot of our carers felt that they had no autonomy as parents, they couldn't make day to day decisions. That was undermining to the carers, but it was also undermining to the children, in that it seemed to reinforce the sense that this isn't quite family somehow, that this is something different. (Adult)

(VCC 2003, p.25)

Young people in the consultation exercise emphasised the need for professionals to respect them and to demonstrate this by keeping appointments with them and by listening to them. Their views on relationships with professionals were that they should be reciprocal, with respect on both sides. Social workers and foster carers should trust young people like they would their own children.

Peer relationships were reported as both positive and negative: close friends were like family, but some reported that other looked after young people 'could bully you and make you feel unsafe'.

Most children and young people identified their families as the people they cared about most, particularly their mothers, relatives and siblings. Most young people reported that it should be easier for them to see their families. For black and ethnic minority children and young people this was identified as particularly important, in that for many of them this was their only connection with other people who shared their ethnicity.

Many young people did not want to be fostered, making a positive choice to be in residential placements. One of the advantages of this was that residential care was seen by them as reducing the conflicting loyalties between birth and foster families.

A 2006 study of looked after children's views was carried out by Morgan, the Children's Rights Director for England. Participants were looked after children and young people, some of whom were care-leavers. Over half the 22 respondents in the postal survey considered that they made some decisions, for example about their social life, but only two had made a decision about their placement choice, although most were consulted about placement moves. The author of the report about the discussion group data found that:

After someone else had made an important decision for them, like a change of school or placement, without involving them in it, huge changes in their lives happened suddenly without much warning or preparation. One child told us how they were picked up from school one day to be moved to foster parents, and had no choice of foster carer and no chance to say good-bye to their mum. (Morgan 2006, p.6)

Overall, children considered that adults and professionals should simply ask children what they think and feel, and really listen to what they say. Most children and young people thought that their placement was 'OK' for them, but some thought that they were 'not OK'. Children said that they should be offered a choice from at least two placements, that their social worker should check everything was going well when they first moved, and that they should be able to keep going to the same school when they changed placement. Being allowed to not hold religious beliefs or to keep your own beliefs or religion was also important, even if your foster family's beliefs were different (Morgan 2006).

The main things that were reported as going wrong in placements were: arguments, fights and being unhappy or depressed. Some placements were considered by the participants as not likely to have worked out anyway. Children felt that they should not have to move far from family and friends, unless it was clearly best for them, for example if they had special needs that could not be accommodated locally, or if they were at risk from someone in their family, but not because of policies or money issues. Three-quarters of young people reported that they had attended the reviews where their care plans were agreed, but only one person felt that he had been able to express everything he wanted to in the review meeting. As a child-centric study, the findings were reported exactly as the participants told the research team, without the addition of adult or professional views. The findings were disseminated free-of-charge in child-friendly language through electronic publication on a children's rights website (Morgan 2006c).

These studies about the care system (Morgan 2006c; Schofield 2000; VCC 2003) demonstrate some of the particular features of looked after childhoods. They did not however consider foster children specifically, but looked after children in general. Children and young people report how stigma, fears and a lack of even basic information can be part of looked after childhoods. They also report that they want to be cared for, trusted and to influence the decision-making about their lives.

Children's understandings of their participation in the care system

The idea of children as service users who have a right to participate on policy issues and services that affect them is a relatively new concept. There have been several studies about children's participation in the looked after children's review system, but not all of these were based on children's views. Shemmings' (1996) study, for example, only considered the views of the professionals, to identify the barriers to children's participation.

Thomas and O'Kane's (1998) *Children and Decision Making* study involved 225 children and young people aged 8–12 years in England and Wales, with children from seven different local authorities. They offered children a choice about how the interview was set up. Some children welcomed the opportunity to be with others in the same situation and so preferred a group interview. Others did not wish to disclose information regarded as personal to them; for these children and young people an individual, one-to-one interview was more appropriate. This study was in three stages, each with its own participatory technique (Thomas and O'Kane 1998). At the first stage, they invited children to set up their own decision-making charts on a large sheet of paper: 'what sort of decisions' for the top axis and 'what people' for the side axis. The grid was useful as it not only facilitated the children's decision-making but also enabled the researchers to explore what issues children identified as important decisions.

The study aimed to explore how children who were looked after away from home were given a say in the decisions made about them. It also aimed to understand how social workers and carers facilitated children's inclusion in the decision-making processes. All the looked after children and their social workers from the seven local authorities were included in a postal survey in the first stage of the research. For the second stage, 47 of those children were interviewed, as were their social workers, carers and some of the birth parents. Group activity days with children and young people were also carried out, as were observations of a limited number of reviews and planning meetings. A number of participatory activities were designed in order to make the research meetings more fun and interesting for children, and to support the engagement of a wide range of children and young people. One of these participatory activities, for example, gave children differently labelled pots for them to place beans in: one pot for a little, two for some and three for a lot. They were then asked how much say they had about particular decisions about differing aspects of participation, such as 'how much I like meetings' and 'how much preparation I get for meetings'. This enabled children to talk about their responses with the researcher as they carried out the activity.

The findings of this study concerned children's involvement in meetings, children's views about social workers and also the ways in which children were included in decision-making. Things that made meetings harder for children were: feeling that they were put on the spot, having their lives discussed by strangers, not knowing who will be there and what would be discussed, and meetings that went on for too long. The things that made meetings easier were: knowing everyone at the meeting, being prepared and supported, being given a choice of how to take part and having time to say what they thought. Some of the professional decision-making had long-lasting consequences for children, such as losing contact with their relations, as this unnamed 10-year-old boy cited in the study explains:

He [the social worker] doesn't care really [about] when I see my cousins.
I miss my cousins a lot that's why... I saw them four years ago.

(Thomas and O'Kane 1998, p.37)

Some children had been involved in their placement moves, but many described the experience as strange and outside their control. When the moves were repeated, particularly those moves that happened without warning to children, this caused them distress and disturbance. The ways in which children were included in decision-making varied according to the following factors: how well the child's voice was heard, how much consensus there was between the child's perspective and the adults' views, the degree of influence which other people had on decisions, the degree of control that adults chose to maintain, the age of the child, the kind of decisions at issue and, last, any perceived risk to the child. Whilst children in Thomas and O'Kane's (1998) study understood and largely accepted decisions that did not accommodate their views, they considered it important for someone to have explained the reasons for this to them.

As part of a 2005 Scottish study of the participation of looked after children, Turpie interviewed 11 children aged 8–12 years (Turpie 2005). The study looked at one part of the decision-making about looked after children: decisions on permanency planning, which is planning for children to remain in the foster care system until adulthood. The study was concerned with how and to what extent children's views were accommodated in the decision-making processes about permanency. Other phases of the same study examined documents and interviewed professional workers.

Five key areas were identified by Turpie as illustrating the tensions between the 'participatory' intentions of current Scottish child-care legislation and policy, and social work practice with looked after children. The five areas were: the way in which the current permanency-planning process is unclear and too drawn-out for both professionals and looked after children, the 'role' played by the Children's Hearing System in permanency planning, adult control versus child protection, the confidence and skill level of social workers and, last, how 'child protection' work took priority over permanency planning.

There were marked differences in the findings from the data gathered from children and that gathered from professionals. Only one of the 11 children fully understood his permanency plan. All 11 children identified their social worker as the key person who had decided that they should be permanently separated from their parents. However, their understandings of the reasons for this were largely confused and blurred. Children largely wanted to attend important meetings, to be involved and given information about their life stories and families. They did not, however, want to hear distressing and/or painful things about their birth families. Children wanted meetings to take place outside of school hours: they wanted to know most of the people who attended meetings about them, and not to be asked questions by strangers. There were general concerns voiced by children that they were only told about important decisions after they had been made, so asking for their views was then irrelevant (Turpie 2005).

Studies in this area demonstrate both the diversity of the ways in which children can be engaged in the looked after monitoring and review systems and their relative lack of success in being listened to by professionals. Positive, trusting relationships with professionals were identified as enabling children and young people to participate effectively in the looked after children's system.

Children's views about support and advocacy services

One of the earliest studies concerned with looked after children's views was a 1994 quantitative study by ChildLine, a voluntary agency who provide a telephone helpline and support service for looked after children (Morris and Wheatley 1994). Stage One of this quantitative study reported on a postal survey of the 539 callers, aged 7–18 years, to the looked after children helpline in the preceding year of 1993. Seventy-six per cent of callers were female and 55 per cent were aged 14–16. Fifty-four per cent were in residential care and 32 per cent in foster care. Forty-six of the callers were interviewed; for those in foster care this comprised 22 children who were fostered: 11 girls and 11 boys. Stage Two considered the 137 children in Scotland who had received support from the ChildLine support service for looked after children, out of the 826 callers to the helpline in the preceding year. Twenty per cent were in foster care and 60 per cent were girls. A postal survey was conducted and 17 children were also interviewed.

When comparing looked after children with children in the general population who used their mainstream service, ChildLine found that looked after children were amongst the most troubled and unhappy children to whom they talked, and also the most alone. Foster children were found to be more likely to report feeling isolated than those in residential care; this was attributed to them having less contact with their peers and less awareness of any support services that might be available to them. A theme was found of children who felt unimportant, unloved, dislocated and abandoned. Children reported that they wanted to be involved in the decision-making about their lives. They wanted abuse to stop, many having reported physical or sexual abuse both before and/or after being looked after. They also strongly resented their confidences being broken, with private information becoming public. Many reported feeling insecure, as Mark, aged 12, explained:

Foster Carers are OK, but they send you back if they don't want you.

(Morris and Wheatley 1994, p.41)

Comparisons between Stage One of the study, in England and Wales, and Stage Two, in Scotland, revealed that none of the Scottish children expressed uncertainty about the reasons for them being looked after, compared to 17 per cent of the participants in Stage One. Overall, children in this study reported wanting to be cared for, protected, respected and encouraged. The children who reported more satisfaction about their carers were those in long-term placements who regarded their carers as surrogate parents and also those who were in short-term placements for specific reasons, such as respite care.

A study by Pithouse and Crowley (2007), commissioned by the Welsh Assembly, examined children's use of an advocacy advice service between 2003 and 2004. The aim was to investigate the nature of children's complaints and their experiences of using the advocacy service. Twenty-two Welsh local authorities were surveyed. From these local authorities, 114 children and young people, who had made complaints and were contactable and willing to participate, were identified. From this sample, 25 children from each of the five different Welsh regions were selected for interview. Nine of the interviewed children were fostered: the remaining 16 were either in children's homes or living with parents or relatives. Twenty-two were white Welsh and three were black British. The complaints initiated by children related to issues of: personal care, how or where they were looked after, contact with birth families, relationships with significant adults and effective communication with staff. Those complaints made by adults, largely birth parents, on behalf of children, differed; the issues were: the quality of provision, decision-making, perceived attitudes and inaccurate or negative recording. Pithouse and Crowley found that the advocacy process was dominated by adult-intimated complaints: those complaints initiated by children tended not to have been proceeded with. There was little effective advocacy to support children who wished to pursue their own complaints (Pithouse and Crowley 2007).

The same themes of children reporting negatively about communication with professionals, about where they lived when looked after and about contact with their birth families were evident in both these studies of support services. Although both studies combined the separate groups of looked after children, the ChildLine study, in comparing the groups, found that children who were fostered were at greater risk of becoming isolated, as children and young people in residential care had other looked after children for support and were more likely to be aware of support services.

Chapter summary

In this chapter studies which have sought to generate the accounts of children and young people about families and welfare services have been explored. As Rowe and colleagues found (Rowe *et al.* 1984), listening to children's accounts and views enhances awareness of the gap between the ideal and the reality of fostering. Children and young people can and do articulate clear opinions and perspectives on the difficulties and dilemmas that confront them, about their families and support services and about being looked after. This message of wanting to be consulted was present in many of the studies reviewed. In general, looked after children reported how they wanted to be cared for by their family or foster family, to be trusted and to influence the decision-making about their lives. Not all children were happy in their foster home; some did not feel safe or trust their carers, and some reported being abused (Triseliotis *et al.* 1995). Reports from young people that review meetings were intimidating (Buchanan 1995; Thomas and O'Kane 1999) appear to persist across time, as this was a common finding in more recent research. Children's feelings of insecurity and their wishes for 'normality' and 'privacy' ran through many different topics.

What is apparent from these firsthand accounts about being fostered is that children and young people can contribute a fresh standpoint to understandings of being fostered. Children's views can help to explain the gap between the aims and realities of fostering. Looked after children and young people are vulnerable and dependent on the vagaries of public care. Ignoring their messages increases this vulnerability, as Hill *et al.* explain: 'The refusal to accept that children and young people are competent witnesses to their own lives has confined them to a state of impotency, at the mercy of adults, some of whom, as history teaches us, cannot be relied upon' (Hill *et al.* 2004, p.84).

Part Two
Setting out the Evidence Base

Chapter 5

What Children and Young People Say about Moving to a Foster Home

Increasingly, looked after childhoods are becoming understood as lacking in permanence, with an acknowledgement that many looked after children and young people will live in several different foster homes (Sinclair 2005). Little is understood about how children themselves understand their moves to and between foster homes. Drawing on a research approach from the sociology of childhood, a study was designed by the author to seek children's views on becoming and being a foster child. What emerged from the data of that study was how children's accounts of being fostered illustrated a high level of anxiety and concern about being moved to new foster homes.

This chapter first looks at the literature about children's moves. It then describes the research study undertaken, before exploring the data generated from children's accounts of their moves to a new foster home. Last, there is a discussion of the implications for research, policy and practice in this area.

Looked after childhoods

Although there is an increasing wealth of research on children's views of being looked after, there has been somewhat less of a specific focus on those who are fostered and very little concerning children moving to foster homes. In the research literature in this area, discussion concerning moving has been rare; when this does exist, the focus is inclined to be on the causation factors for moving such as fostering breakdown rates, as in Quinton et al.'s (1998) study of children in long-term placements.

Sinclair et al.'s major study (Sinclair et al. 2005) found that only one in six of their sample of 596 long-term foster children had managed to achieve permanence. Only a quarter of the children in this longtitudinal York study had remained with the same foster carers for three years. Continuing foster care was linked to age, with younger children more likely to be adopted or in kinship care. Those children remaining with the same foster carers were predominantly aged 4–14. Those aged 14-plus were likely to move to independent living, with only 10 per cent of those aged 18-plus remaining with their foster carers. Moving on can, therefore, be considered as a normal aspect of being a foster child.

A child-friendly research design was used by Thomas et al. in their 1999 research study which explored the opinions of 41 adopted children in England. The mean age of their sample was seven years; the youngest child was aged five. Thomas and colleagues found that children had often found the preparatory explanations of adoption difficult to grasp, reporting that they had been worried about moving, about what would happen and the changes that they would have to face. For some children this was allayed by information about their new family being conveyed in a way that they could understand. Many children and young people were reluctant to be uprooted from a home where they felt settled, as one 9-year-old girl explained:

> I didn't want to move. I wanted to stay with [my foster parents] 'cos I'd been moved around so much.
>
> (Thomas et al. 1999, p.33)

A 10-year-old girl, also from Thomas et al.'s study, had experienced 17 previous placement moves, which had resulted in her losing most of her possessions. Here she explains how this occurred:

> I usually lost things. I didn't have many, many things because I kept on moving and they were usually stuck up in the attic, so I forgot them. So I didn't really have anything that moved.
>
> (Thomas et al. 1999, p.58)

The limited amount of fostering research which includes research with children, rather than research about children, tends to consult children on adult-selected topics. This includes, for example, studies such as Cleaver's study concerning contact (Cleaver 2000) or Thomas's study about children's participation in reviews (Thomas 2005), which were funded by the DOH, to consider areas that were policy relevant.

A 2006 study of looked after children's views was carried out by Morgan, the Children's Rights Director for England, concerning looked after children and young people, some of whom were care-leavers, foster children or were receiving children's care services or living away from home. Using postal questionnaires, discussion groups and a survey conducted by texting on mobile phones, participants' views of placements, decisions and reviews were gathered. Only two had made a decision about their placement choice, although most were consulted about placement moves. Morgan reported that:

After someone else had made an important decision for them, like a change of school or placement, without involving them in it, huge changes in their lives happened suddenly without much warning or preparation. One child told us how they were picked up from school one day to be moved to foster parents, and had no choice of foster carer and no chance to say good-bye to their mum. (Morgan 2006c, p.6)

Children said that they should be offered a choice from at least two placements, that their social worker should check everything was going well when they first moved, and that they should be able to keep going to the same school when they changed placement (Morgan 2006). Some placements were considered by the participants as not likely to have worked out anyway. Children felt that they should not have to move far from family and friends, unless it was clearly best for them, for example if they had special needs that could not be accommodated locally, or if they were at risk from someone in their family, but not because of policies or money issues.

Discussion of children's views of moving have been sparse, and limited attention has been paid to children's moves to foster homes. What literature there is about moving does not arise from research that focuses specifically on this topic, but rather tends to emerge from general research about children's views of being looked after.

Theoretical approach to the study

In essence, the research approach utilised in this study is one informed by the sociology of childhood. The sociology of childhood enables children's lives and experiences to be studied in the present. This has particular advantages for researching with foster children, who can largely be considered as temporary members of a foster family (Sinclair 2005). The view of children as competent reporters on their own lives is central to understandings within the sociology of childhood. This differs from other research models, where children are often considered as unreliable witnesses (Qvortrup 1994). Both the sociology of childhood and research with children share the same principles: namely (1) childhood is a social construction; (2) childhood (like class, gender, ethnicity and age) is a variable of social analysis; (3) children's social relationships and cultures are worthy of study in their own right; (4) children are active in the construction and determination of their own social lives and the lives of those around them; and (5) children are not simply the passive subjects of structures and processes (Winter 2006, p.60).

A child-focused perspective must acknowledge the distinctive cognitive and social developmental characteristics of children (Christensen and James 2000). Child-focused or child-centric research methods are here understood as those which strive to minimise the power differentials between the adult researcher and the child participant, which use appropriate communication mediums and which are primarily concerned about researching *with* children, rather than researching *on* them. Children are not a homogeneous category, with many differences within and between chronological age categories and individual childhood experiences.

Effective communication with children may lie in the use of modes of communication which are more comfortable or enabling for some children, for whom the use of written and verbal communications in formal language could be experienced as excluding and unhelpful. For young children, play is often a more natural medium through which they can express themselves, with drawing, acting and the use of stories and metaphor becoming understood as valid forms of self-expression, which can be usefully employed when researching with children. The methods used for this children's views study attempted to accommodate varying attention spans and language skills.

Research design

I initially decided to interview 15 foster children from each of two different local authorities, in an attempt to minimise bias from any localised and particular organisational fostering practices. Semi-structured interviews were selected as an appropriate research tool for the exploration of highly individualised accounts of sensitive issues for vulnerable children and young people to recount. The words chosen by young people to illuminate their 'tensions, dilemmas and pain' (Gilligan 2001) are key to understanding the accounts of the lived experiences of fostered children.

Qualitative data were collected by the use of interviews, using a narrative approach to the interviews, with additional prompts and more detailed requests for information in some instances (Elliott 2005; Wengraf 2000). This choice resonates with approaches in oral history and feminist research, concerned with giving respondents their own voice (Wengraf 2000). Participants were also asked if they wanted to draw pictures of their family; this proved popular with the younger participants, although several of the older teenagers declined. Some participants gave less detailed responses at interview than others, for example both the participants with moderate learning difficulties gave brief, but quite thoughtful and informative, responses to most questions, and with one other respondent I seemed unable to establish a rapport sufficient to generate an in-depth interview. Most of the interviews, however, generated unique insights into highly individualised childhoods, but additionally communalities also emerged in the data. The use of open questions enabled the respondents to explain and recount areas and issues that were of concern to them, some of which I had not anticipated. Overall, the interviews were complex, frustrating and time-consuming to arrange, set up and transcribe, but generated rich and interesting data.

Sampling

The sampling frame was selected as volunteer fostered children between the ages of 7 and 16, the justification for the age restriction being that the participants should have sufficient verbal skills to express clear opinions. I chose to interview only children who were currently fostered, as much of the existent knowledge base of fostering is reliant on reflective accounts of people previously fostered or proxy accounts of fostering from professionals. I used my own networks, from previous work as a Children's Guardian, to negotiate permissions from local authorities to approach parents and children.

The correct ages of the participants have been maintained, but their names and those of their carers, social workers and any places they mentioned have all been altered by me, for reasons of confidentiality.

Description of sample

The characteristics of the interview sample are presented in Table 5.1.

Table 5.1 The characteristics of the interview sample

Interview total	Gender	Age (in years) at interview	Local authority	Ethnicity
22 (from 19 different foster homes)	7 male	1 aged 9	12A	3 black
	15 female	1 aged 10	10B	1 mixed-race
		5 aged 11		18 white
		1 aged 12		
		5 aged 13		
		3 aged 14		
		2 aged 15		
		2 aged 16		
		2 aged 17		

The initial target sample size for the interviews was 30, selected as appropriate for a one-person research project with limited resources. In practice, 22 became a feasible sample size given the lengthy process of recruiting from a difficult-to-access research population. At this stage of the interview process the data were, in any case, proving to be relatively consistent with similarity in the themes arising from the data.

The age distribution was clustered at 11- and 13-year-old children. The youngest child in my study was 9 years old. This was not an oversight, but as a result of the methods chosen and my lack of confidence at the beginning of the study in collecting and interpreting younger children's views. I had intended to include young people up to the age of 18, but few older teenagers volunteered to be interviewed.

All 12 of the children from local authority A were white British, with six white British from local authority B, three black British and one mixed-race British. One of the white British respondents from local authority B self-identified as Irish, in common with her long-term foster carers, but had actually been born in London and had British nationality. Of the 22 participants, one boy and one girl were identified as having moderate learning disabilities; one other participant attended a school for children with behavioural difficulties and one a pupil referral unit. The remaining 18 largely attended mainstream schooling, with several reporting long periods of exclusion or home tutoring currently or in the recent past.

Fifteen respondents were female and seven were male. The over-representation of girls in this sample is largely attributed to sexism in the referral process, with several social workers making comments about how girls would enjoy talking to researchers, such as 'she really likes talking about fostering' or 'she enjoys being listened to'. This apparent sexism also worked to exclude male participants, with a social worker saying, for example, 'oh, he doesn't like stirring up the past' or a foster mother saying 'he's so busy with his football and college, he wouldn't have time to talk to you'. The inference appeared to be that being prepared to talk to a researcher about personal issues was not something all children would welcome.

Data themes
The following five sub-categories or themes about moves were identified from the interview data:

1. the process of being moved to a new foster home

2. information about the new foster home

3. the emotions connected with moving

4. loss of people, community, networks and possessions

5. the strategies and skills involved in moving.

The process of being moved to and between foster homes

Accounts of the process of moving were varied, but nearly all of the 22 participants had discussed this at interview, some in considerable depth. Most children recollected several moves. Several children and young people reported that their move to a foster home had been sudden and unexpected. They recounted how their first move had been a shock for them, an abrupt intervention in their daily routine. Beatrice, aged 11 and with moderate learning disabilities, talked about leaving her mother and siblings the previous year:

> They just came to school and took me. They just took me…that was Sandra [social worker], really strange, really upset.

Daniel, also aged 11, had similarly experienced a sudden move:

> No, it was decided on the day, I was supposed to be here for two weeks but it turned into long-term… The social worker decided, then the social worker had to rush off to another meeting, so Chris, it was a man called Chris, I can't remember his second name, just took me.

Most of the children recounted several moves, often recalling the sequence of these moves in a matter-of-fact manner, as 11-year-old Freddie recounts when explaining his previous placements:

> I've lived in four other places… I went somewhere, then back with my mum. Went somewhere, back with my mum. Went somewhere, back with my mum. Went somewhere, back with my mum. Four times. The last one was too far for my mum, they had to move me back here.

Children who had moves for which they had had some preparation typically recounted these moves more positively. James, aged 13, recalled how he had been happy to move to his current foster home some years previously. This was his third placement.

> I just remember coming for one day to see if I liked them, but no more, that's all. I felt right at home, right away… We [James and his social worker] came down on the train and we had lunch here.

Some of the participants were experienced movers, and appeared quite pragmatic in their attitudes towards moving. Catherine, aged 13, told me that she had been in at least 15 different foster homes since leaving her family home a year previously. Most of the moves had been quite sudden:

> **Catherine:** I didn't even know I was coming here. I've been here a week… I come home one night and seen my bags sitting in the hall and she just said 'you're moving' like…and so they just sent me off, and I went…things weren't going too well…

Interviewer: So you must have been a bit surprised?

Catherine: No, 'cos I knew I was going to go from there anyway... I just want a bit more notice, tell me a bit early, the day before or that day or something like that... I just don't want to come home and find my cases in the hall. And her saying 'you're moving'. Jane [current foster carer] don't kick no-one out, if you want to go, you go.

Not all of the participants had negotiated a move or waited to be moved; two of the 13-year-old girls told me how they ran off from foster homes where they were unhappy, for example Olivia:

Interviewer: And how many places have you lived in?

Olivia: I think 26, yeah, about 25. All around Bosford.

Interviewer: So, were they just meant to be for a few days?

Olivia: Yeah, no, they was meant to be my carers, I was only there for a few days, they didn't work out, and then I went, you know what I mean? I ran away to my mum's, I always went to my mum's, my sister's, so... I hated the people I was with, awful, horrible, but I like it here... Yep...

Evangeline, aged 14, who had moved 'five or six' times over the last two years, had developed a strategy of giving the new foster home two weeks' trial, before running away if she didn't settle in well:

I suppose you get used to it [moving in with a new family]. If I'm not used to them after two weeks, I'm out of there!

Sixteen-year-old Stephanie, who had recounted five moves, had been privately fostered at a friend's house for several months, but felt that the situation had become untenable:

Everything just went wrong from there and I was getting moody, like, and there was a girl I didn't get on with there and we just fought and I was just getting more violent, like, and I just thought, tell the social worker, so she come round later and I just got to move. And I got moved to Haley's.

Overall, the process of moving can be considered as a variable experience, from the unexpected removal for which the child had seemingly no prior warning, to well-planned moves and, for a small minority, moves that were instigated by the child themselves.

Information about moving to the new foster home

The amount of prior information participants reported knowing about their current foster home varied considerably. Fourteen-year-old Laura had found out that the planned two-week respite turned into a long-term foster placement:

> I wish they'd told us we were going to live here, not just going for a visit.

Nine children knew nothing about their move; some children had filled the vacuum with assumptions that distressed them. For example, here's Laura again, recounting a move when she was eight and her thoughts on the long drive to a foster home she knew nothing about:

> No-one said anything before, they just come and took us from school. The social workers like, they never told us, they just said you're going to stay with these people for a couple of weeks...and we've been here ever since, and that was years ago, when I was eight, and Matthew...run off and they got him another day... I thought it would just be all adults and that no-one would speak to you like.

Four other children knew a little about their new family; they all reported knowing or remembering details such as which animals the new family had. For example, 13-year-old Olivia only knew on the day of moving that she had to leave her then foster carers, but did get given some details about the new family:

> [I knew that] they...was called Jane and John and I was just coming. I knew they had two cats.

Some children had multiple-move experiences which included different types of preparation; for example, Arthur, aged 12, had had an earlier move that he attributed to his behaviour, specifically that he and his brother had been fighting.

> Uhm...I knew that I had two sisters and uh...two dogs and two cats... Uh...I received a video tape, a recording of them... I had pictures...a family box... No, it was alright... I find it alright here, I think it's better than the other foster place, I've lived in three places, in the first place me and my brother was together, but then we started fighting and the woman said she couldn't handle it. She phoned social services... And we broke up, and we went to individual carers.

The reason for the move was also reported as a concern by several children. Some children reported that they had been given explanations for the need to move that they had not believed, as Kylie, aged 11, recounts:

> **Interviewer:** Who told you about coming here?
>
> **Kylie:** Sally, my social worker, she sat down and she told me...yeah... huhm... Yeah...she showed me a book and she said that there isn't

enough space in the house. That Auntie Carla's looking after too much children...but I think that's not true.

Interviewer: What do you think was true?

Kylie: I think that they didn't like me and Auntie Carla just said... huhm...

Eleven-year-old Freddie, when recounting his previous foster placements, had also received an explanation for his move from home and seemed similarly sceptical about the plausibility of this explanation.

Freddie: I don't know why I had to go. Deidre [social worker] said it was to help my mum cope [he looked really tearful at this point]. We're in care until we're 16. I've got five years, Aaron's got seven, Ben's got 12 years and Carl's got 15 years.

Interviewer: Is your mum coping better now?

Freddie: Yes, but we're still not allowed back home.

So, there was a marked variation in the amount of information and prior knowledge of moving to a new family, with the largest group, nine children, reporting that they knew nothing about a new foster family. Several of the children seemed preoccupied with wanting or needing to know the reason for the move, and two of the participants reported dissatisfaction with or did not believe the information that they had received.

The emotions connected with moving

Moving away from a home where they were settled to go into a new family was a time of intense emotion for many of the respondents: feelings of injustice, rejection and being scared, bewildered or upset were widely reported. For some, moves were talked about in a more pragmatic way, in a resigned, realistic and accepting manner. Those children who had welcomed the idea of leaving a problematic situation still talked about how they were apprehensive about how the new family and home might be: about leaving the familiar for the unknown or largely unknown. The first move into care was often recounted as the most frightening. The tension, or wariness, reported in some accounts contrasts with those where children reported feeling more comfortable about the move, which they typically attributed to circumstances such as prior meetings with foster carers or being reunited with siblings in the new foster home. Harriet, aged 12, moved to long-term carers whom she had previously visited:

I was scared, 'cos I'd left my old foster carers. I'd been there a long time, a couple of years... I was about nine... We came here and stayed for about two weeks, like a holiday, then we went back and got ready to live here… It was OK, [but] if you get settled in a home and family, it's unfair if you have to move and change school.

Beatrice, aged 11 and with moderate learning difficulties, told me about moving to her foster family four years previously and, despite having moved there with an older sister and now being happy, had at first been lonely:

It feels like you're all alone and you've got no-one to talk to but yourself.

Some moves between foster homes were recounted in a less negative manner; for example, Kylie, aged 11, had rather complex feelings about her move:

Interviewer: Were you a bit worried about moving?

Kylie: Well, I was happy inside…on the outside. But I just needed to show emotion…'cos my friends was there and I was going far away and I didn't know no-one…that was at my school in Westfield. They came on a really nice day…yeah and the Xbox. Yeah, I felt right at home because I got to know them already.

Some people don't understand how sad the children feel and they just won't listen, and they just feel like everything's alright and the child's saying that everything's alright, but they could be really upset and not just showing it like. And the parent would never know about it, unless the child confessed.

Olivia, aged 13, also explained a concept of having to be careful and on guard:

Just be aware, always alert, just be polite…things like that. I was in my room a lot. I was in the shower a lot. I went back in my shell.

For the foster children who lacked a trusting relationship with their carers, moving had brought about, or increased, a sense of isolation, as 13-year-old Natalie relates:

Interviewer: Do you talk to them when you have a problem?

Natalie: NO, I don't talk to anyone. It's not worth it. It only gets me in trouble.

The respondents were seemingly aware of the nature of the foster carers' attitude towards them, of the conditionality and therefore vulnerability of their place in the new household. This status of conditionality, as well as a lack of familiarity with the home to which they were moving, meant that the move was often associated with tension and the necessity to be alert and watchful.

Loss of people, community, networks and possessions
For many of the children, their losses were not separated out into component parts; it was the familiar life that had been lost, for most children to be

replaced by life as a foster child in an unknown family. The children and young people in this sample were aged 9 to 17 years old, ages when a normative experience is of growing independence, with some autonomy of movement in places that are local and familiar. Natalie, aged 13, explains how she did not know where her new foster home was.

> **Natalie:** Well, we got lost on the way here, we was driving round and round. Diane [foster carer] come and picked us up in the car, well, we followed her.
>
> **Interviewer:** Did you feel at home?
>
> **Natalie:** Not really, no, being in someone's house again. Somewhere where you don't even know where you are.

Matthew, aged 17, recounting his move into foster care some six years previously, had been moved from a run-down inner-city housing estate, where four generations of his extended family lived, to a small-holding in the country:

> Yeah, but I didn't want to go. It would have been real strange like. I just didn't want to go, that was my life, like... Horrible. I just missed my family. Gutted... I just come and I needed to be alright. I just wanted to run back, you know?

Laura, aged 14, is Matthew's younger sister and at the same foster home. Matthew elected to be interviewed separately, telling Laura that she had to 'go' first. Laura described how the sudden move had scared her:

> I was scared 'cos it's a long way in the car and I thought 'how will I get back?'

These three accounts of Natalie's, Matthew's and Laura's all illustrate a feeling of being geographically dislocated, of losing a sense of familiarity with their neighbourhood. For some children, the turbulence of their lives, with sudden moves, resulted in repeated losses of things that were important to them. This links with Jackson and Thomas's definition of continuity for looked after children, as applied to the child's networks of relationships, their personal and cultural identity, and their education and health care (Jackson and Thomas 1999, p.19). Stephanie, aged 16, talked about two earlier experiences of loss:

> Well, I lived with my nan and granddad then. I lived with my nan until nan died. Yeah, I miss my cats and that. After I left, my granddad gave the youngest to upstairs, my mum took Tibbie, and Jessie run off... 'Cos of things that have happened, I can't live in a house with men. When I got chucked out [from a previous foster home, when aged 15], they just took my stuff to Margaret's place. I was told there was one boy and

there was three, plus her own son and her husband, who was really vicious though, there was no way I was staying there. No way. I stayed there for supper and then I went out. She said 'you are coming back aren't you?' And I said 'no way' and I just slipped out. I left all my stuff there and just went.

Olivia, aged 13, advised that care needed to be taken to keep one's own possessions safe:

Keep care of your own...stuff gets nicked.

Harriet, aged 14, accepted that there was a risk of losing contact with her parents, and advised new foster children to try to avoid this risk:

If you have a choice, keep in touch with your mum and dad... Don't be scared.

For most of the participants, moving from their original families to foster care meant that their family life and daily routines had been replaced by occasional contact with some of their immediate family. Thirteen-year-old James told me of contact with his siblings:

James: Well, my brother Charlie, he's older, but I'm not sure how old, and Emma lives at home, she's one. I see Connor whenever I ask, like in the holidays, he's four and he's adopted.

Interviewer: Do you see them as often as you want?

James: Just Connor. I see the others every six months.

For some foster children, promises at the time of moving, to keep in contact, had been eroded over time, causing long-standing resentment, as 13-year-old Olivia recounts.

Interviewer: Do you get to see the people who are important to you?

Olivia: Yes. Mum and Dad, I can see them, but it's once a month contact. I see my dad and my sister at the moment...but not Mum, I'm really cut up about it... I hardly ever see my brother uhm...yeah, so, that went off quick...

Interviewer: As often as you want to?

Olivia: No, I got the stupid social workers to thank for that. I don't see my mum, at least three times a week, I don't see my dad at least once a month, I don't see my brother at least two times a week. URGHHH!

In summary, most of the participants had faced losses in consequence of the move to foster care. Some had been relieved to leave aspects of their previous lives, and most had continued with a relationship with some members of their immediate family. Several were concerned about losing close contact with some family members, with losing pets and belongings, and with the loss of friends and/or neighbourhood.

The strategies and skills involved in moving

From the participants' accounts, a 'looked after' career appears to provide children with a growing sense of what to expect in a new foster home and how this might be managed or coped with. Some experienced movers seemed rather detached from the process, almost proud or defiant about managing what was seemingly a rejection from their current home. Olivia, aged 13, advised direct action:

> DON'T GO! Refuse to go! God! My first time of going in to care was horrible! Yeah, there was these kids called Graham and Terry, they was horrible, they got this ice and they lobbed it in our bedroom at us, they got this ice machine on the fridge, and they just got it, they was well out of order, we was like fresh meat! Me and Natalie, we got our pocket money and we was straight out of there, we got the first bus. We were like 'Mum, get the tea ready', like you do, I don't even drink tea. It was well funny. They thought they was nice to us. I thought, yeah, well.

Both Elizabeth and Freddie were more experienced movers having had several changes of foster carer. Freddie, aged 11, had tried strenuously to avoid being separated from one of his brothers, but was ultimately unsuccessful:

> At first, I was in my other care home, when I first found out. I was home with my mum and my social worker Tracey said I had to go to a fourth place, and so we ran off... Me and my brother. Yes. They found me at my aunt's, I thought I was going with my brother, I was OK with that bit, when my social worker told me it wasn't, I was in the car, my brother was getting in a different car, he was trying to get in this car, he started kicking and punching Tracey to get in... I was kicking the door, trying to get out...
>
> Tracey was holding my hand and Aaron's [his brother], she said 'do you want to go on your own?', we stamped on her feet to run off. We went to Bedford, we weren't really allowed that far, but I didn't care. We went on the bus. That was a scary experience... My mum was pleased, we thought we were going to be there for another day, and then Tracey came. That was at my aunt's.

Elizabeth, aged 16, had adopted a strategy of avoidance by absenting herself from the foster home except for sleeping:

> My first placement, and the others, they didn't last that long... I was moving around for the first six months and then I came here. My first

placement, I didn't get on. I'm not racist or anything, but I didn't want to come in, they eat different food to what we ate and that, I didn't want to come in. The other foster kid was black, I was the only white person there and I didn't feel that comfortable. I just got up, got showered and went out.

This strategy of avoidance was reported by several other children, often exacerbated because the foster carer refused to leave them in their home unsupervised, or because they refused to attend school. Sixteen-year-old Stephanie, at age 15, had spent most of the day wandering around:

She [foster carer] used to go out in the mornings at seven thirty, eight o'clock and I had nothing to do, I didn't have a school or anything, so, until my friend got in, I just hung about. I just used to get a bus to London and back, I didn't eat anything, I just used to go to bed and get kicked out in the morning...

You don't know people, you don't know who they are. Just 'cos they're under social services, it doesn't mean that you can trust them.

Natalie, aged 13, had adopted a 'look and learn' strategy for coping with the arrival at a new foster home:

When we got out, we unpacked the car and carried things in, and before we were in the door I was like WATCH and we had some dinner, but I didn't like it and Diane [foster carer] made me beans on toast.

Olivia, aged 13, was mindful of the need to avoid difficulties, and remained alert and polite:

Beware of the kids...just be aware, always alert...just be polite...things like that.

The use of new technologies offered the potential for new strategies to circumvent the local authority social workers' attempts to control family contact. Communication was facilitated for some families by the use of computers and mobile phones. Laura, aged 14, recounts how she now managed to talk to her father between visits:

Laura: I talk to my dad on the computer.

Interviewer: Oh, is that often?

Laura: No, not really, 'cos it's a new thing like, he's only just got the computer.

Georgina, aged 15, advised new foster children to adopt her own strategy for being able to talk freely with her parents:

Take a mobile phone with you, to keep in touch with your family.

The underlying difficulty that these accounts reveal is that of moving to live with a family you do not trust, of having to develop a strategy to negotiate the unfamiliar people and routine. Avoidance, by absenting oneself or 'going back into my shell', seems to be the strategy used by the more experienced movers.

'Don't be scared'

The most frequently cited response about how to improve fostering was for children not to be scared when they move. When asked what advice they might offer new foster children, 20 of the 22 children interviewed said that they would tell them not to be scared or afraid. Thirteen-year-old James considered that it would be helpful for children, when they first went into a foster home, to know that they would still see their birth parents:

James: Don't be scared. The people are usually really nice.

Interviewer: What might be helpful for them to know before they go there?

James: That they're still going to see their mum and dad, not to be scared.

James identified the potential discomfort at having to live with strangers and offers a sensible strategy to overcome this. As James's account explains, difficulties can be about missing your 'real' family.

Nine-year-old Daniel gave the following advice for newly arrived foster children:

Don't really worry, try to be friendly, and try to get on with the other children, to mix with other people outside.

In summary, most children and young people reported feeling isolated, scared and at times overwhelmed when they joined a new foster home and they did not feel able to share those feelings with others.

Discussion

The use of a research design that drew on the sociology of childhood sought to capture children's own accounts of being fostered. Through the use of open questions in semi-structured interviews, topics that were of importance to the participants emerged. The strongest theme in the data from children's accounts was of them wanting to tell me about being moved to foster homes. This was surprising, in that I had anticipated focusing on how children settled in foster homes.

One thread ran through all these accounts: of children and young people's powerless position in relation to the key players involved in decisions to move them to foster homes – social workers, birth parents and foster carers. One of the ways that these data on moving can be understood is through the theoretical consideration of the sociology of childhood, with children seen as social actors, not just in reporting their individual views and experiences, but also as co-constructors of those experiences. In each sub-theme there were accounts of how children had, on some occasions, been overwhelmed by moving. Other accounts showed how children had exercised agency to avoid the new family by strategies such as absenting themselves from the home during the day or more drastically by running away from the new family. Children had their own views about what they wanted to happen, but largely lacked the resources to act on those views.

Three types of move were described by children: those that were sudden, those about which the children had some prior knowledge, and those that had been well planned. Two children had experienced only one move, but most children reported several moves. One 13-year-old girl who had moved many times considered that moving was not a bad experience, she just wanted some notice. 'Well-planned' moves were those where children received the type of information that they wanted before the move, and they had an opportunity to visit, stay with or meet the carers beforehand. Not all information was accepted unconditionally by children; some children reported being sceptical about the information or reason for the move that they had been given by social workers or carers.

Although children were able to exercise their own agency in some situations, in others they had no voice. This links to central concepts from the sociology of childhood, as described in Chapter 2, where children were considered as a minority group (Mayall 2002). There were many accounts of situations that illustrated looked after children and young people's position as a relatively powerless minority group (Mayall 1996). In contrast, social workers appeared to make decisions on their behalf. Utilising Fox Harding's (1998) model of child welfare, this can be understood as state paternalism. Using children's understandings of themselves as dependants who have to obey adults, and who identify power as lying with adults, Mayall (2002) argued that children form a minority social group, a category of persons who lack power. When decisions are made about children and young people who are looked after, their rights are often marginalised. Their lack of information about where they had been moved and lack of practical resources, such as money and mobile phones, rendered children relatively powerless. Gaining familiarity with a situation and acquiring resources enabled some children to exercise agency.

In the accounts children gave of moving to foster homes, these themes of a lack of agency, of not being consulted or listened to and not being able to act were played out in many different ways. Both the Children Act 1989 and Article 12 of the UNCRC (UN 1989) grant children the right to be consulted: to say what they think should happen when adults are making decisions that affect them, and to have their opinions taken into account. Moving to a new foster home could be considered to be a major decision that affects most aspects of children's lives. The model of fostering that was illustrated in the data does not demonstrate support of children's participatory rights in social work practice, at even the lower levels of Hart's typology of participation (Hart 1992).

In the analysis of children's accounts of moving to and between foster homes, a portrayal of the complexity of moving families and the very different ways in which these moves take place has emerged. Experiences seemed very varied, both within and between the two local authorities where the study took place and also both within and between the individual accounts of the child participants.

From the accounts of moving portrayed in this chapter, moving can also be considered as potentially problematic for children, possibly also potentially placing them at risk. Young people of 13 and 15 reported that they were wandering the streets until it was bedtime, rather than spend time in a new foster home where they felt uncomfortable. Sinclair's study also revealed that the characteristics of foster carers seemed linked to placement stability, with kindness, firmness and being slow to take offence identified as characteristics that supported children in achieving long-term placement stability. This finding is potentially complementary to my data, in that these characteristics could be linked to facilitating trusting relationships between foster children and their foster carers. If so, carers who are kind, firm and slow to take offence could be those who facilitate a successful negotiation of the initial tense, awkward early stages of the foster family relationships reported by several participants.

Whilst fostering relationships are traditionally evaluated by use of psychological understandings, with a reliance on attachment and social learning theories, other considerations may be useful in making sense of children's reported experiences. Moving to a new family is here understood as a varied, somewhat haphazard experience, which children try to negotiate warily. For some children, prior meetings have facilitated a trusting relationship with the new carers, enabling the move to take place in a positive manner. For others, the early suspicions were allayed and stable relationships established. For yet other foster children, trust with the new family was not established and multiple moves became the pattern of their care career.

The use of sociological explanations enables factors other than parental attachment patterns to be considered as contributing to understandings of how children move to and negotiate foster families. Children may or may not be seeking alternative parental attachments, but some, conceivably, could be merely looking for comfortable 'lodgings' or even a 'house sharing' type of relationship with the foster family.

Chapter summary

This chapter introduced the author's own research study, with data from 22 interviews with children and young people who are fostered. The research approach drew on the sociology of childhood, which recognises children as valid commentators in their own lives. Sociological explanations can facilitate a wide exploration of the relationships and organisation of fostering. Enhanced understandings of the dynamics of the fostering process and the relationships experienced by foster children have been gained through the exploration of accounts from children who are currently fostered.

The use of a narrative interview technique enabled children and young people to explain their experiences and views of fostering. For some children being 'taken' from their school to live with strangers was a traumatic event which they could recount in great detail several years later. A key message from the foster children interviewed was that their moves to foster homes were often frightening events. Five aspects of the moves were significant in the data:

1. the process of being moved to a new foster home
2. information about the new foster home
3. the emotions connected with moving
4. loss of people, community, networks and possessions
5. the strategies and skills involved in moving.

Despite children's rights to be involved in decision-making about them (Children Act 1989; UN 1989), the data demonstrate examples of both good and damaging social work practice within both local authorities in this study. This highlights an ad hoc approach to best practice and a widespread disregard for children's rights. The lack of integration between national welfare policies for looked after children and the procedures and practices of children's services (Bullock 2006) is also evident in the findings from this study.

Chapter 6

What Children and Young People Say about Living in a Foster Home

Introduction to children's reports of living in a foster home

This chapter is concerned with how children reported their experiences of living with foster families, drawing on children's accounts from the interviews conducted by the author in the research study described at the beginning of the preceding chapter. Most of the 22 children and young people interviewed expressed mainly positive attitudes towards their foster carers, but some had experienced difficulties with either their current or previous foster carers. Considerations about their foster homes fell into four distinct areas: a sense of belonging, evaluations of foster carers, provisions available in the foster home, and finally how children 'fitted in' to their carers' lifestyle. Most of the children and young people with whom I researched could identify both positive and negative aspects of their current foster home. Sometimes they also referred back to previous foster homes in which they had lived.

Belonging

Distinctions in the recent research literature between types of foster homes, such as Sellick's (2006) distinction between fostering as supplementary care or alternatively as substitute care, echo that of several children and young people in this study. Whilst it has been a useful concept in understanding their descriptions of being fostered, my data demonstrate a variety of responses to membership of the foster family, with several distinct sub-groups. Figure 6.1 illustrates the variety or pattern of belonging which the participants identified.

Some participants, for example, reported that they felt part of both their birth family and their foster family. Some children reported a transient lifestyle, with little sense of belonging to any family or carer.

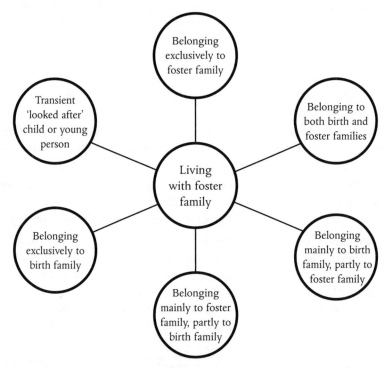

Figure 6.1 Pattern of reported belongings

The structures and proscribed roles of fostering and foster family membership, as outlined in Chapter 1, create a complex situation. If their child has been accommodated by the local authority on a voluntary basis, then the birth parents retain their parental rights for a child, who is deemed to be temporarily living with carers who are not parents. If their child has become looked after through a court order, then the birth parents share their parental rights with the local authority. In essence, children belong to a family with whom they no longer live and live with a family to whom they don't belong. What, however, is the lived experience of children and young people who are fostered? They reported highly differing ways of belonging to either, or both, their foster and birth families, or, for some children, of not belonging. Their own accounts have several strands running through them: of identity, of love or emotional ties, but also of foster children and foster families struggling to establish their group or family identity.

Membership is used here to encompass some or all of the legal, social identification, domestic and emotional aspects of being in a family. Belonging is used to articulate the respondents' own identification as to which family they were part of. In negotiating dual membership of both birth and foster families, many respondents often made reference to both families when describing their foster family.

Transient children

Some of the children and young people's reports about fostering were marked by an absence of belonging. Some respondents described not having links, or having only tenuous links, with birth families, but of also not belonging in their foster home or rapidly changing series of foster homes. Thirteen-year-old Catherine had experience of many different foster homes. She mainly appreciated her current foster home for being accommodating of her busy social life. Catherine had told me about her frequent moves of foster home and how her friends and her older boyfriend seemed to be the people she trusted:

> No, I don't see none of my family, my mum and stepdad or my family any more, just my sister and my real dad...
>
> Jane [current foster carer] don't kick no-one out, if you want to go, you go. But here I've got my own key. I come in any time I want, especially on weekends, on Fridays or Saturdays. She isn't most probably here all the time, she's out most probably. I'm not allowed to bring my friends in if she's not here.

Sixteen-year-old Stephanie had lived in several foster homes and had had changes of social worker. She had acquired some expert experience of being a looked after child, gained during the last seven years, and was sceptical about care professionals:

> Foster carers and social workers, they don't know nothing. You don't know people [foster carers], you don't know who they are. Just 'cos they're under social services, it doesn't mean that you can trust them.

This links with another part of the author's research, with a discussion group of care-leavers. Seventeen-year-old Bella, from that discussion group, also had little trust in carers. She explained that, whilst children and young people could rely on foster carers to provide food and a bed for them, being safe and protected was not a given, but was conditional on having good foster carers. Bella told the group:

> All you can say is that they will give you food and a bed. You don't know if it will be safe.

Other children and young people in the fostering interviews had also acknowledged that some foster carers exploit and abuse children.

Belonging exclusively to a foster family

Nine-year-old Queenie is the only child of a recently deceased single-parent mother and she has no close relations. She reported feeling close to her foster sister, Ruth. Queenie is white and Ruth is one year older and mixed-race, having a black Nigerian mother and a white British father. Queenie found her claim of sisterhood sometimes challenged by the obvious ethnic difference between the two of them:

Interviewer: How do you feel about being here?

Queenie: I feel OK, 'cos it's nice and we're staying here 'til we're 18. Only 18 and we will still visit her... I say uhm, I just say Ruth's my sister. If they ask, I say no, we say we're cousins.

Fourteen-year-old Trevor has moderate learning disabilities and a speech impediment, but when drawing a family picture, he explained clearly how he belonged with his foster family:

All us? I got big family. I got another family, but I only part of this family. All my brothers and sisters.

Sixteen-year-old Veronica was also settled into the same foster home as Trevor. She had changed her surname to that of her foster carers and chosen to stop seeing her birth relatives several years ago. In response to a question about what sort of things worried her she said:

Veronica: That people will find out about me being actually fostered. No-one knows about it, even my best friends don't know.

Interviewer: Who knows about this?

Veronica: Just my mum and dad, fostering, people in the house and my aunties and uncles. They all know, but they all treat me as if I'm the same. I'd rather people didn't know. 'Cos they really treat me as their daughter. They'll be asking me questions and they'll be all 'Aah', they'll really be treating me as...they'll be different or whatever...

This enduring membership of a foster family has been reported in the fostering research literature. This has resonance with Schofield's findings from a retrospective study, that in adult life many former foster children still saw themselves as part of their foster family (Beek and Schofield 2004).

Belonging mainly to foster family, partly to birth family

Fourteen-year-old Evangeline had had experiences of feeling that she did not belong to previous foster families, but was settled with her current carer. Going away on a family holiday was reported by her as an indicator that she belonged to this family:

> **Evangeline:** It's different to other placements. Tracy will never replace my mum, but it's different. I don't know, I can't explain it. It doesn't feel different. It's not like you're fostered, you get involved with everything they do, it's not like you're fostered, it's like you're one of the family... We only went to Butlin's so far, but if Tracy goes away, you do too, you're not put away or anything, you're included. You're part of the family.
>
> **Interviewer:** Was that the same in your other foster homes?
>
> **Evangeline:** No, you're in the way, they're getting paid, not me.

James, aged 13, described his foster family to me:

> **James:** Yes, they're Stella and Phil. Yes, they've got two of their own sons called Ben and William and then they have a person called Stephen who's like my oldest brother, I really like him, he's really cool. And a person called Carl, but he passed away, I didn't know him...then a person called Alan, he's really cool, then my brother called Matthew, he annoys me sometimes, just 'cos he's a little brother... Ben and William aren't foster children, but the others are. Stephen, like he's 27, and he still classes them as Mum and Dad, and Alan's 19, he's still here.
>
> **Interviewer:** Oh, are they both still here?
>
> **James:** No, Stephen works on the cruise ships. He didn't go back. I'm going to stay here too, I'm not going back.

Seventeen-year-old Matthew explained how his 18-year-old brother had moved to a flat in the nearby town:

> Yes, he's moved out now, he's gone. Yeah, but we're not really apart, he's down here all the time and I stay there.

Some of the foster children reported feeling that they were a permanent part of their foster family. Three of them, including Matthew, who is quoted above, illustrated their future with reference to an older sibling or foster sibling who had provided them with a model of a route to how their future, their path to adulthood and independence, might happen. All three of these respondents had also talked about birth relatives with whom they had regular contact, but saw their future as part of their foster family, even in adulthood, when they would be living independently.

Belonging to both birth and foster families

Several children reported how they accommodated membership of both their birth family and their foster family. For some, this duality caused tension, with concerns about their birth relatives appearing to have an impact on their feelings about belonging to the foster family. Fourteen-year-old Ursula was happy living with her foster carers, but this was balanced by concerns that her mother and sisters might not be as fortunate in their circumstances, as she explains:

> I'm worried about not being with my mum…and my sisters. I know that I have good care here, but I don't know about them… This is a nice place and I like living here. It's not like any other foster home… I got a big cheque for my birthday, I bought clothes and jewellery. They care about me… I feel happy about living here.

Farmer and Moyers (2005) differentiated between 'stranger foster care' and 'kinship foster care'. Only one of the interview respondents had previously known his carer, as he was fostered by a teacher from his previous school. The remaining 21 respondents were all fostered by families or individuals previously unknown to them.

Belonging mainly to birth family, partly to foster family

Eleven-year-old Beatrice considered her foster home in a positive way, in that it was a good place to stay. In response to a question about the best thing about living with her foster family, she clearly identified herself as belonging to her birth family:

> **Beatrice:** Yes, that it's [fostering] kind people who seem to care about other children whose families haven't gone really right.
>
> **Interviewer:** And the worst thing?
>
> **Beatrice:** That I'm not at home. Not in my own home. Missing my mum and my sister and all that.
>
> **Interviewer:** What sort of things are different?
>
> **Beatrice:** You haven't got your own family around and they don't kiss and cuddle you and that.

For Beatrice, the absence of affection within the foster home was the main distinction made between the differing relationships she had with her foster family and her birth family. Not feeling loved or cared for in the same way as with her birth family illustrates the difference for Beatrice between belonging to a family and being cared for by a family.

Belonging exclusively to birth family

Thirteen-year-old Olivia explained to me that, although she liked living with her foster carers, she only had one set of parents. This was despite the fact that she had not seen her mother for six months, because of a family argument.

> **Olivia:** I been here a year, and it's quite good here, I like it, it's MY home. It's MY house. I'm a bit funny with the kids. There's other people [other foster children] that come in this house, but I like them. Anne and Dave think I want the house to myself and that I don't like the other kids, but that's not right, I don't. I'm not always used to them, they're not always here for that long, they're here for about a week or so, then go, here for a week then disappear, but anyhow...huhm...

> **Interviewer:** What do you call your foster carers?

> **Olivia:** Anne and Dave. I've got a mum and dad, so... My mum and dad, or my mum, would get very angry if she found out that that, I, I, I, I, [stutters] that's my mum and dad. Anne and Dave, so, friends with them. No, no, but, if they passed away, that would be another story, but, they're here, so... I've got a mum and dad, that's hard, so that's it... As they are still here, they would be angry, so they're still around, I've still... I've already got a mum and dad...and if Anne doesn't mind, so you only get one mum and dad in this world, only one mum and dad, no replacements, which I think is fair enough.

Thirteen-year-old Natalie, Olivia's identical twin, who lived in a different foster home, also firmly believed that she only had one set of parents:

> I'm not calling them mum and dad because you only have one mum and dad and that's it.

Some children reported a lack of acceptance at being a looked after child, and also at having to live away from their birth parent. Whilst this did not seem to affect their evaluations of their foster home, it did seem to have an impact on their sense of not belonging to their foster family. Eleven-year-old Freddie explained in the previous chapter on moving about how he had been removed from home by the police, after running off in an attempt to stay with his mother. Here he recounts how he had joined his foster family the previous year:

> **Freddie:** I went to another home, a temporary one, until they could find me another place.

> **Interviewer:** What did you know about Janice and Len before you came here?

Freddie: I knew she used to teach in year ZZ in my old school. I, I didn't know nothing about her, but that she was a teacher person. I'd seen her before. I felt upset because I'd already fitted in with them [previous carers].

Interviewer: Can you explain to me about fitting in?

Freddie: It's quite easy, 'cos I've got a good sense of humour and I can take a joke.

Interviewer: What is it like living here?

Freddie: It's quite nice actually, now. And I fit in at my school now. I used to lose my temper, I used to think people were taking the mickey 'cos I lived with my teacher and not my mum. I thought they crowded around and took advantage.

Interviewer: Are there many rules?

Freddie: Yes, quite a few rules. Washing my shoes. Doing homework. Things like that.

Interviewer: What happens if you break them?

Freddie: I havn't ever broke the rules. I've been taught that you don't muck around in other people's homes.

Freddie's understanding of foster homes as 'other people's homes' illustrates this theme of living with a family to whom you don't belong.

What is apparent from these accounts is how children make their own sense of their family situation and have clear ideas about where they belong. Interestingly, none of them mentioned or referred to the legal status of their situation, or any explanation that social workers or carers might have given them.

Children's evaluations of their foster carers

In Chapter 3, I noted that the characteristics of carers are considered as a key factor in the success of fostering placements. Carers who are warm, clear, firm, understanding and not easily put out are identified by Farmer and her colleagues as having lower-than-expected rates of placement breakdown (Farmer *et al.* 2004). Being available to offer support to foster children in ways which they find acceptable potentially enhanced placement stability. Several of the interview respondents reported positively that they had a carer who was kind, generous and explained things. As noted in Morgan's study (2006a), respondents reported quite consistently that they were not informed about moving to foster homes, or the reasons for the move. In this information vacuum, carers who explained things were seen by children as being particularly valuable to foster children. When foster children are worried or upset, they valued having a foster carer who listened or was supportive. Four of the 22 children and young people who were interviewed mentioned this as the best thing about being fostered. Some children had spontaneously included being 'a good listener' in descriptions of their carer.

I asked 10-year-old Ruth what made her happy:

> Donna [foster carer] is what makes me happy, she takes us out and she gives us stuff and she talks to you and she explains things and supports you and things.

Nine-year-old Queenie lives in the same foster home as Ruth and is also positive about their foster carer:

> **Interviewer:** Do you feel that your foster carer cares about you?
>
> **Queenie:** Yes, she does care about me. She knows I'm fussy about things like homework and she does it. If you're sad, you can talk to her any time. She's nice and she cooks nice food. She takes us places every weekend… And she is…kind and she…you can talk to her if you got a problem.

Eleven-year-old Kylie had had several different foster homes, but seemed happy and settled with her current carer. Like Ruth, she was appreciative of a foster carer who explained things. Her perspective is referenced against an earlier adverse experience of foster care, when she reported being wrongly accused of lying. Kylie and her foster carers were all black British Afro-Caribbean. Kylie referred to all her foster carers as 'Auntie', with the use of fictive kinship terms being usual within black Caribbean families (Reynolds 2006).

> **Kylie:** But I like Auntie Rhonda, she makes me feel comfortable…when I'm naughty, when I don't clean my room, she does know. But she doesn't call me a liar. Like Auntie Anna [previous foster carer]…there was some tissue paper balls on the wall of my room and I didn't do it and she called me a liar…that's why I love Auntie Rhonda, she listens to me…she listens to what I have to say too and if she ever thinks it isn't true…if she thinks I'm telling a lie…she knows when I'm telling a lie and she knows when I'm not telling a lie and she loves me always and her family's just so nice.
>
> **Interviewer:** Do you feel that they help you when things are difficult?
>
> **Kylie:** Yes, they help me with my learning, they find out things for me…and they talk to me when I get confused…she explains to me in a kind way, she explains it step by step. Well, she says my mum is ill, she's under tension and she's still not recovered from her illness…

William, aged 16, also appreciated having carers who listened to him:

> That they cared a lot and that when I needed to speak to them they were there to talk to.

Having a foster family that you respected was also valued by some foster children. Seventeen-year-old Matthew had told me about how his birth parents had had serious substance misuse problems, which led to criminal activity, imprisonment and the family splitting up. His foster parents, in contrast, had a close extended family and were relatively successful, running a small family business. Here he talks about their work ethic:

> They're [foster carers] always working, they're alright, yeah. They don't quit. They keep on going 'til they finish something. Eileen is always on her feet. Always.

Matthew's 14-year-old sister Laura appreciated the same foster carers for differing reasons:

> Eileen and Keith, my foster parents, they make me happy. They're really nice and kind… Well, I remember they gave us presents when we come… I was still crying over my mum and stuff, but I soon got used to it.

Sixteen-year-old Veronica was also settled into a long-term foster home, where she had lived since she was a baby. Veronica had changed her surname to that of her foster carers and chosen to stop seeing her birth relatives several years ago:

> I'm very proud of my family [foster family]. I like doing things with them, having them around, big barbecues, things like that… They really treat me as their daughter. But in this family, if we're in the wrong, we'll say, same as Mum and Dad, everyone respects each other, like.

Frances, aged 13, particularly appreciated her foster carer's generosity. Frances was the only girl in her foster family, with a foster carer who told me how she really enjoyed finally having a daughter to shop for. This experience contrasts with Frances's position as one of four daughters in her relatively impoverished birth family:

> They are always nice to me and they spoil me… Clothes and jewellery, Sally [foster carer] buys me new things all the time. Being nice to me and spoiling me and stuff like that.

Fourteen-year-old Evangeline is now settled in a long-term placement. She has had several previous placements and describes below the difficulties that arose in two of those earlier placements. For Evangeline, trust, or the absence of trust, was a key element to her evaluation of her relationship with carers:

> **Evangeline:** But the others, they were only doing it for the money. If they went out, you had to go out, there was no trust or anything. My first placement, and the others, they didn't last that long… I was moving around for the first six months and then I came here… At one

of my placements, they had locks on their doors, on their daughter's door, but no locks on the foster children's doors. But it feels like, when their daughter's got locks on her doors, there's no trust, they're only doing it for the money.

Interviewer: Oh, did you feel that they were trying to lock you out?

Evangeline: Well. It couldn't have been any other way, there's no locks, there was a lock inside, so I got changed, but they had locks inside and outside, and if they went out, you had to go out too. They got up and went out and you had to go too.

One of the young people in the discussion group differentiated between good foster carers and foster carers who were celebrated by the local authority. Eighteen-year-old Bella reported that good foster carers were those who really cared:

Good foster carers, the ones that care with their hearts, aren't celebrated. Those ones that jump in the limelight, they're rubbish, sometimes.

The young people interviewed often talked quite objectively about some of the carers' personal qualities, but the younger children tended to relate the qualities to their own needs. Typically the younger respondents would link a positive quality to how it impacted on them, for example 'she's nice and she buys me things'. The qualities most important to the respondents were generosity, listening, explaining and being supportive.

Provisions available in the foster home

Some of the respondents appreciated the amenities by referencing them to earlier situations of adversity which they had experienced. Most respondents evaluated what was distinctive about the current home from the relatively well-informed standpoint of having lived in several different families. Six of the interview respondents lived in the same foster home as another respondent, i.e. three sets of paired foster children, two of whom were a sibling pair. The children in the same placements largely identified different factors to those identified by their foster sibling, indicating that evaluations were made from individual perspectives.

Many foster children commented positively on provisions made for them by the foster carers, or on aspects of the foster home which they enjoyed, such as pets, toys or leisure facilities. Trevor, aged 14, reported being happy and settled with his carers, but the best thing for him was receiving new computer games:

Good. Get everything I want to. Games. Lots [of] games. And other things.

Eleven-year-old Arthur enjoyed having space to play in. He asked for his foster mother to stay with him during the interview. He attends a school for children with behavioural difficulties and he and his foster mother talked about how, at times, he finds his moods difficult to manage. Arthur's foster family encourage him to go outside and 'take it out on the garden', as he explains below:

> I've got half an acre of back garden to play in. I've got loads of toys. Uhm…more toys…I don't know really… I just like it here…yeah and my bedroom, it's small, but it's all England. You know, football. England wallpaper, England duvet and all that… What was it? [rhetorical], about three weeks ago…I really kicked off didn't I, and then I started breaking my toy car up, and John [foster carer's brother] come up and said 'Why don't you go and pull some weeds up?' and I went out and pulled a whole load up… I was thoroughly enjoying it like…

Thirteen-year-old Michaela lived in a rural foster home. She identified some positives about her foster home, saying that overall it was 'alright', but also some difficulties, which are explored in the next sub-category:

> **Interviewer:** And what is the best thing about living here?
>
> **Michaela:** The horses, dogs, ferrets, that's it.
>
> **Interviewer:** And do you get to do nice things?
>
> **Michaela:** Riding and going out places and things like that.

Georgina, aged 15, and her 12-year-old sister, Harriet, live in a foster home in a small village. In response to a question asking 'What is the best thing about living here?' they both identified practical issues:

> **Georgina:** It's the garden, the trampoline, being near my mates and school.
>
> **Harriet:** Yeah, it's being right in the middle of everything. And having nice food and things.

Eleven-year-old Daniel was also appreciative of a central location, particularly at living near his school:

> I wake up at twenty to nine, get dressed, get my breakfast, and just go. Go straight to school, it's just around there [points through window]. And I get privileges, like the Xbox and TV in my bedroom.

Fifteen-year-old Unity considered that the best thing about her foster home was a combination of amenities and having other children to talk to. She advised new foster children to make the most of their opportunities:

I live near the town, we have a trampoline and a pool in our garden and there are other kids here to talk to… Stay strong and try to make the most of opportunities.

For 14-year-old Stephen, the positive change for him was more play:

Play more. Get to stay up more.

Provisions were mainly reported in a positive sense, with the only negative reports concerning allowances. Allowances are awarded by local authorities and indirectly paid to foster carers, for them to pass on to fostered children at their discretion. Unlike other provisions, which are arbitrarily made in the sense that they relate to the foster carers' lifestyle and standard of living, allowances can be considered as an entitlement.

Fitting in with the carers' lifestyle

This category is concerned with the social aspects of joining and/or living with a foster family. Whilst most of the literature is preoccupied with the emotional and psychological aspects of substitute family life, the respondents seemed to also report the social aspects of the foster family as being significant. Reports of feeling excluded by social difference, or 'bridging' the divide, seemed to be how children understood and described negotiating the social location, or categorisation, of this substitute family. Respondents in Morgan's (2006c) study of young people in care reported that being allowed to not have religious beliefs, or to keep your own beliefs or religion, was important, even if your foster family's beliefs were different. Fifteen-year-old Georgina and her 12-year-old sister, Harriet, explained to me how church attendance was compulsory for the younger children in their foster family, but Georgina was now considered old enough to make her own choice on this matter:

Interviewer: And the worst [thing about living in the foster home]?

Harriet: [Emphatically] Church and that stuff… They're Christian, so they do things differently, you got to go to church and all that.

Georgina: I don't have to go no more, I just go out with my mates. I'm not allowed to have my mates here when no-one's in.

Discipline was an area of concern for several children, with harsher discipline reported as being particularly resented. For 13-year-old Natalie, both the severity of the punishments in her foster home and the low level of pocket money were problematic:

Interviewer: And what sort of things do you get in trouble about?

Natalie: Being mouthy…and swearing…that's it.

Interviewer: And what happens when you get in trouble?

Natalie: I get put in my room for a week. Yeah. I go to school but I'm not allowed out to play. I'm allowed out to the toilet, but I have to have my dinner in my room, you're not allowed to chat, you have to stay in your room. Yeah.

Interviewer: Do you think that your foster carers are fair?

Natalie: No. Punishments and stuff like that. Pocket money, I get a fiver, I mean, I'm thirteen! That's it really.

Eleven-year-old Arthur was also critical of the punishments in his last foster home, which he had left 18 months previously, after two-and-a-half years there. He also had not been happy about being sent to clubs and holiday play schemes, where he said that his 'bad behaviour' caused problems for him. Here, he compares the two foster homes, in response to a question about whether or not the rules in his current foster home were the sort of rules he was used to:

Yeah. It was more stricter at my last carers. I was there two-and-a-half years, but I was only supposed to be short term. People here aren't so strict… They did it [sent him to holiday play schemes and after school clubs] without my consent, basically, they never really asked me, they just sent me. I do like scouts, 'cos that was a new thing for me. It was a bit different at the other foster carers… If I was naughty at school, they used to send me to bed, at 4 o'clock, they'd call me down for dinner and then send me up again. I was only 7 or 8.

Arthur's account of a lack of consultation or agreement about how to spend his leisure time meant that living with a family where organised activities were part of the routine became problematic for him. For 13-year-old Ursula, the care of her sister, Yvonne, who is ten years younger than her, had created problems in an earlier foster home and had led to Yvonne being separated from her in the current foster home. Fostering is often organised around age groupings, with foster carers having marked preferences for children of particular ages, although for emergency placements children can be placed in the only available placement, rather than a matched placement. The fact that carers may have a lifestyle that does not easily accommodate the needs of particular age groups can preclude sibling groups remaining together. Yvonne had been moved from the current foster home, a situation Ursula recounted in a matter-of-fact way:

Ursula: Three places. I've lived in three. I was staying at Auntie B's for two days and it wasn't really satisfactory. It was shit, I didn't really get on with her. And Yvonne was a small baby then, but I had to look after her, she was in my room and I had to see to her in the night as well. Auntie B didn't do nothing for her…

Interviewer: Did you come to visit this foster home before you lived here?

Ursula: Well, it was the day my mum took us to Brighton, it was the night. Well, I was quite upset, 'cos we'd just been taken [removed by the police]. So I didn't really fit in at first, 'cos I was so upset. Yvonne was a bit unsettled, but she couldn't really say anything. My sister [Yvonne] was here. She's been gone, about a year. Because Auntie, she's brought her kids up and she wants to work.

Ursula's explanation, of being too upset to fit in at the start of her placement with the second foster family, links fitting in with being emotionally ready to fit in. Being upset or unsettled precluded her and her baby sister from fitting in with this new foster family, although she subsequently settled down and reported being happy with her foster carers. For some children, marked social differences were seen as a barrier to integration in their foster family. Sixteen-year-old Stephanie, who is white, had been placed trans-racially, with black foster carers, on two occasions. Although she conceded that the first black foster family were 'nice', the racial difference was seen by her as a barrier to being a part of the family:

My first family, the Walkers, they were black, they were like private foster, and it was rude, because you were like the odd one out, you weren't part of their family. I knew Carla, from school, she was alright. And they were nice, they took me to their church and showed me how to cook nice food, but I didn't think it was allowed, that you could have different cultures, different races and everything. It's happened to me twice now, 'cos Janice was black. The issue wasn't race exactly, it didn't bother me, but I didn't think it was allowed. When I was with the Walkers, it was like an emergency. I don't know if other kids make it easier, it does depend on how much trust you got.

Reported difficulties did not include factors such as any lack of provision, but were largely those arising from relationships with carers. The power of carers to discipline in ways that the respondents clearly considered unacceptable, or not trusting foster children to be alone at home, or to have their friends at home without adult supervision, were reported by several children as problematic. One foster child, Arthur, linked fitting in with negotiating, or in his case not being able to negotiate, how the differences might be bridged. On the other hand, not all aspects of fitting in were negative. Fourteen-year-old Evangeline had moved several times, but told me that she was now settled and happy. She, too, was appreciative of the freedom offered in this foster home:

Other foster placements, they don't give you so much money. They're pretty generous here. And there's no rules about meals and things. Obviously the kitchen's closed, there's no proper cooking then. I have to be in at half ten, I'm not allowed to cook something proper then, but I can microwave something.

They're not really after your money or anything, you can come in when you want. If we're all in, Zena [foster carer] will cook something, but it doesn't happen often. I can cook my own dinner. Zena does my washing and that, I just have to clean my room. That's all I have really got to do. I didn't have chores, to do much in my other placements, but to be fair, I weren't really there that long to know the rules and that.

Evangeline's acceptance of the prohibition on late-night cooking and belief that in this placement the carers are not financially motivated is interesting. Some foster children mentioned money in terms of feeling that the fostering allowances were either the incentive for 'carers' to offer them accommodation, or that their allowances were misappropriated. This withholding of clothing allowance was included in the earlier section about provisions.

Whilst many of the children in the interviews had been critical of their treatment by social workers, or about the process of being moved to foster homes, none of them described being fostered as a chance to get away from their previous lives.

Chapter summary

Children and young people told me about their individual sense of belonging to a family: some of the foster children reported feeling that they were a permanent part of their foster family. Other children reported that they were staying there but belonged with their birth family. Some reported belonging with both families, whilst some young people worryingly appeared to have few ties to either family. This last group would appear to be particularly at risk of social exclusion.

Most of the children and young people reported favourable evaluations of the new lifestyle that they had acquired through membership of their foster family. They appreciated such things as good amenities. Some children reported problems they encountered with their new lifestyle, such as being disciplined in ways which they clearly considered unacceptable. Not being trusted was also considered problematic.

The accounts from children and young people about belonging to their foster family resonate with Sellick's findings, in that fostering was either supplementary care, or substitute care, in relation to the care given by birth parents (Sellick 2006). This indicates that the ongoing role of the birth parents, or possibly the child's wishes or expectations in relation to the ongoing role of the birth parents, may be a causal factor in children's understanding of their position in the foster family. Some of the key messages have resonance with findings from other research with looked after children. Some children in the author's study had seen attendance at religious services as problematic, when they did not share the foster family religion. The discussion groups reported in Morgan's (2006b) study found that children and young people thought that they should not have to change or acquire a religion to accommodate a foster family's beliefs; it should be acceptable to keep your own religion or to have no religion (Morgan 2006b).

Overall, children and young people formed individual understandings of their situation, with little apparent awareness of their legal status and their rights or entitlements. Whether this situation will change with the new *Care Planning, Placement and Case Review* (England) regulations of 2010 (DCSF 2010) remains to be seen.

Chapter 7

What Children and Young People Say about Fostering Systems

This chapter is concerned with how foster children report their experiences of fostering services. I have argued, in Chapter 2, that foster homes are provided as a public service, within which children attempt to lead private family lives.

For looked after children, parental responsibilities are shared between birth parents and local authorities; the discharge of those parental responsibilities is located within the bureaucratic process of corporate parenting. This is regulated by central government, but interpreted in each local authority or children's trust by local councillors, policy officers and social work managers.

The views of children and young people set out in this chapter came largely from my 2009 research study, as set out in Chapter 5. There are two sets of issues examined: the first explores children's understandings of the fostering system; the second considers foster children's suggestions for improvements that might be made to fostering. Children and young people largely made a clear distinction between social services departments and the professionals, usually social workers, who discharge the parental responsibilities of those departments.

Children's evaluations of the fostering system

The way fostering is organised in practice was described by several children as impinging on their family life as a child in a foster family. Aspects of the overlap between the regulation of public services and the usually private lives of families have a direct impact on the lives of children who are fostered. Fostering agencies, for example, have the power to remove children; there are restrictions placed on foster carers to regulate the way they treat foster children and there are complicated bureaucratic processes involved in identifying, planning and responding to the needs of individual foster children. Foster children, as subjects of the public law which legislates for and regulates their care, are indirectly controlled by the policies of social work agencies, largely through the auspices of social workers. Foster carers are accountable to fostering agencies, which include local authority, private and voluntary fostering agencies. The regulation of individual foster homes is determined by a combination of national policies, for example those concerning discipline (DOH 2002), and those determined by the individual fostering agency, for example the rates of pocket money (Broad 2008).

There was a wide range of opinion expressed by children in their evaluations of the fostering system. The fostering system was variously reported by children as being welcomed, accepted or resented. Not all respondents agreed that children should be fostered; from the 22 interview respondents, three respondents thought that fostering should be 'banned' and four others reported that fostering should be 'more like normal family life'. Four themes stood out: feelings about being fostered, fostering as a public identity, a lack of power, and trusting foster carers. Each of these themes is separately considered within this section.

Eleven-year-old Freddie, despite reporting that he liked his foster carers, thought that fostering should be 'banned'. Fostering, as a solution for parenting difficulties, was not an option with which he agreed:

> **Freddie:** I don't like fostering. I don't really think it [fostering] should be brought up in the system.
>
> **Interviewer:** Do you think other things should be done when mums are finding it a bit of a struggle?
>
> **Freddie:** Yes, give them parenting tips. Yes, it would help giving them tips and not going into care. No, just ban it.

Not all respondents considered being looked after as a negative experience. Fourteen-year-old Trevor was quite positive:

> **Interviewer:** What makes you happy?
>
> **Trevor:** Being in care, being at the club. My games.

Thirteen-year-old James was also positive about fostering: he thought that he was largely treated in the same way as a child in a 'normal' family. His concern that being looked after might be like being 'shut away' was not his own experience, but he thought it was a possible outcome, as he explains below:

Interviewer: What is the best thing about living here?

James: It's the freedom you get, you don't feel like you're being shut away or anything. They just treat you like a normal family or something... And there's lots of benefits, like the computer, and it will usually be an easier life. 'Cos you're going to have people there, like a mum and dad and social workers, people who look out for you.

Eleven-year-old Beatrice wanted foster carers to treat foster children like their own children, but also acknowledged that wanting to be part of a foster family depends on whether or not a child wanted to be 'in care', as she explains below:

Beatrice: Make it [fostering] as, more like home. Like the way they were living at home.

Interviewer: Can you give any examples?

Beatrice: To act like the people they were living with before, kind and caring and to treat them like their own child... It depends if you should be in care in the first place, not everyone wants to be.

Beatrice's view that not all foster children want to be 'in care' was shared by other children in the interview sample, who reported that they did not need to be fostered.

Thirteen-year-old Olivia considered that the matching of children to foster homes should be an important part of the fostering process. She had been fostered in several foster homes, initially with her twin sister and subsequently separately, but was now happily settled in her current foster home:

Interviewer: What could be done to make fostering better for children?

Olivia: I think foster workers should match children up to the right family, so that it should be a process, so they can say, right, that's the one they should match them abc, they should stay there one night and they should watch them so it's not, 'I can move you, I can move you', it's like suitable... Yeah, I'd say, kids should be matched up with the right person, there should be more visits.

Not all the children interviewed talked about fostering in general; most talked about their own experiences of individual foster homes. Those that described fostering as a process had clear ideas about what should be done to improve this process, whether it was matching children to the right family or acting like the people the child had lived with before. Turpie (2005) identified tensions between the intentions of participatory policies and the practices experienced by the children the policies were intended to support. The data in this study, however, demonstrate how children's views can contribute to the knowledge base of fostering, by bringing a fresh perspective and firsthand accounts of the difficulties of not being appropriately matched to a family.

Stigma: the public image of children who are fostered

Some respondents chose to keep their identity as a foster child private and went to great lengths to protect this confidentiality. They indicated a perceived stigma about their care status, which they sometimes avoided acknowledging socially. It did not seem to be the fact of being in care per se that was problematic, but the reaction of other people if they knew children were fostered. Fifteen-year-old Veronica had changed her birth name to that of her foster carers by deed poll, but had found that some aspects of her identity were difficult to keep private. She had been fostered with the same family since infancy and had used a strategy of secrecy so that she did not have to deal with the implications of being seen as a looked after child. Here she explains an incident when her 'cover' was breached:

> You have letters like at school, it said once, like, foster parents or carers, like I nearly died that day, I thought that someone might have seen it. I don't think anyone did, but as soon as they have that sort of information… Plus, like if anyone needs, like, a social worker to sign it. 'Cos I changed it [surname], I made a big fuss, 'cos I'm like Veronica Murphy [pseudonym] and I had, I had to go abroad with the name Cormack [pseudonym]. 'Cos when my name was changed, they stamped the name Murphy and they couldn't really see it, so I couldn't get my passport. I can get it now, but I didn't have any proof then and we had to change the name on the booking. I was gutted really.

For 11-year-old Freddie, the fact that he was fostered by a teacher at his own school was public knowledge. This had caused him some problems in the playground, as he explains:

> **Interviewer:** What is it like living here?
>
> **Freddie:** It's quite nice actually now. And I fit in at my school now. I used to lose my temper, I used to think people were taking the mickey 'cos I lived with my teacher and not my mum. I thought they crowded around and took advantage.

The status of being a looked after child is one that can stigmatise children as being different. This theme of being fostered as something about which other children might taunt you was also mentioned by 11-year-old Kylie:

> I would say…if you're being bullied about your foster carer, if they're saying, saying if your mother isn't ill and she abandoned you, you have to go and tell the teacher, not keep it a secret. The boy said that I was abandoned like.

Two young people from the discussion group also reported difficulties in keeping their care status private. Eighteen-year-old Andreas, who has one black and one white parent, found that his placement with a black family meant that he had to work hard to keep his carers away from the school, so that the difference between him and his foster family was not seen. He explains below some of the difficulties he encountered in keeping his care status private:

> I didn't change school. It's hard keeping things private at school though, I just pretended I wasn't in care. If you look different from the foster family, like a different colour, everyone can see, you have to avoid people seeing them. I used to make excuses to keep them out of school, it was hard.

Seventeen-year-old Bella had found that strategies aimed at supporting looked after children educationally had breached her confidentiality, as she explains below:

> On the computer records, that all the teachers can use, it flags up that you're looked after. It's hard 'cos it's not confidential. I'd been expelled from school, but later I went to a PPR [Pupil Referral Unit].

This echoes the work of Schofield (2000), who found that looked after children had to cope with playground taunts such as 'at least my mother didn't abandon me'. Barnardo's (2008) research study found that over half of the looked after children in their study had been bullied in the playground because of their care status. Both Freddie and Kylie were still at primary school and had moved into their foster home during the last year, with their care status apparently known in the playground. Older pupils had reported encountering difficulties when attempting to avoid having to face the public consequences of others knowing that they were looked after. All five accounts indicated that this status had negative implications for looked after children, a status that they strived to avoid becoming public.

Feelings of powerlessness: children's reports of fostering regulation by agencies

The way children reported that fostering agencies prescribed and regulated their care often included a perceived marginalisation of children's opinions in the plans that were made for them. This sub-section concerns the decision-making about children's lives that happened in the public arena and how this determined issues that were important to the respondents, such as contact with parents. Sometimes meetings were held which included the child, but this did not mean that they were listened to. Generally meetings were reported as just a routine event or even as an intrusion. Five of the 22 interview respondents said that either meetings should be banned, or that there should be fewer meetings. Arthur commented that fostering meetings made him feel 'un-normal'. Thirteen-year-old James said that the meetings and processes of fostering seemed to make him feel different and uncomfortable. He points out that his discomfort is about being different, rather than being worried about not living with his birth family:

> Interviewer: Is there something that you think should be done to make fostering better for children?
>
> James: Yeah, well, not so many social worker meetings. 'Cos you feel like you're fostered. And...I can't say exactly, 'cos they make you feel fostered. It doesn't upset me, it just makes me feel different. And check-ups [compulsory annual medical check for looked after children] all the time... Well it makes me feel uncomfortable, like I'm not with my family, but being fostered. It doesn't worry me, just makes me feel different.

Reports from children and young people about social workers' decision-making, for example to determine family contact, were often accompanied by an apparent frustration or resentment that children's own opinions had been disregarded. Ursula, aged 14, was living at an address kept secret from her mother, who had previously removed her children from a foster home without social work permission. The interviewer had been sworn to secrecy about Ursula's address during the arrangements for the interview. Ursula, however, was concerned about not having enough contact with her mother, as she explains below:

> Interviewer: Do you see the people who are important to you as often as you would like?
>
> Ursula: Not really, but that's down to social services.
>
> Interviewer: Who do you feel close to?
>
> Ursula: My mum.
>
> Interviewer: Do you see your mum regularly?
>
> Ursula: No, not really. It's supposed to be monthly. She's not well. But it's not always her fault. I can tell right away. If when I see her, the first thing she says is, I haven't called to [visited] her, if she says I haven't called to her, I can tell right away, how she is, how she behaves. If she's a pain, I just ignore her. How she's behaving. But I don't see her often, I just ask her how she is, keep it short. She did come to the last place and took us. We went to Brighton for the day with her. It's a secret [location of foster home], so my mum don't find out where we are. But I know she wouldn't hurt us.

Ursula's confidence in her own evaluation of her mother's potential behaviour, based on her experience, does not appear to have been considered in the planning of contact or in respecting her mother's parental responsibility. Three other respondents reported that they bypassed official decision-making channels and made their own contact arrangements, which either social services and/or foster carers knew about or were private/secret arrangements. The three respondents who reported this were all from local authority A, were all female and fostered near to their homes. One of these respondents, 13-year-old Catherine, described contact with her sibling that she did not want her mother or step-father to know about:

> **Catherine:** No, I don't see none of my family, my mum and stepdad or my family any more, just my sister and my real dad…
>
> **Interviewer:** So you see your sister. How old is your sister?
>
> **Catherine:** Fifteen. She lives with my mum and my stepdad. I don't see her that often. My sister's not allowed to see me, she comes and meets me. Because she doesn't want to stop contact with me. She makes up a story she's going round my nan's and meets me. Because she wants to see me.
>
> **Interviewer:** Oh, is that your own arrangement or do the social workers know?
>
> **Catherine:** No they don't. It's private.

Catherine appeared to have rejected the formal decision-making processes and made her own informal arrangements to see her older sister, away from adult scrutiny.

Kylie, aged 11, was aware that social services could just come and take you away, for example if you upset your foster carer. She talked about feelings of insecurity that were engendered by her position as a foster child and also about the strategies she employed to avoid having further moves:

> And if you like your foster carer you are happy like, don't get yourself in trouble, don't make her angry or him angry, behave and like they might adopt you or something, and if you like the foster carer they might love you too. They could just phone social services and they could take you away and you could end up in a worse place.

Fourteen-year-old Ursula also considered that the permission needed for children to participate in normal activities should be delegated to foster carers. She made a link between the day-to-day parental responsibilities that foster carers discharge and parental rights about making decisions on the child's behalf, seeing both as a matter of trust:

Interviewer: How would you make fostering better for children?

Ursula: Well, if I was to stay at a friend's house, they have to have a police check, which isn't very nice. I think it should be up to your carer, you trust them on a day-to-day [basis], so why not let them decide?

Sixteen-year-old Stephanie resented the fact that, when her previous foster carer had withheld her weekly clothing allowance, this had not been rectified when she brought the issue up at the review meeting held to monitor her progress in the new placement:

And I got moved to Emily's [foster carer] and she nicked all my clothing allowance… I was supposed to have eight weeks' clothing allowance when I was there; she still owes me about six weeks. We had a review and everything and I mentioned it, but I never got it.

This links with data from the discussion group, where both Andreas and Charlotte explained how meetings were only concerned with negative behaviour by children and young people, not about upholding children's rights by regulating the behaviour of adults. Twenty-two-year-old Charlotte considered that social workers should check that children and young people were receiving pocket money and clothing allowances, as determined by fostering agencies. The rates of these allowances are determined in the public sector and are usually considered by young people to be quite generous allowances, but paid to the foster child indirectly, via the foster carer, as part of the foster carer's payments. Here Charlotte explains how her first carer had withheld most of her pocket money and clothing allowance. She now considers that social workers should check that children's rights to these allowances are upheld:

[Social workers should be] checking that children and young people are getting their pocket money and clothing allowances. Some of them [foster carers] just keep it. In the first place [placement], I only got about £20 the whole time I was there.

Charlotte also considered that the meetings focused on negative behaviour: unless there were problems to be resolved, the meetings were rushed and usually ignored the positive aspects of the progress that had been made by looked after children:

When things are going well, they just do the meetings really quick, no-one is interested. Good things get lost.

Eighteen-year-old Andreas, also from the discussion group, had adopted a strategy of keeping difficulties private: once issues are aired at a review meeting they become a matter of public record and therefore enter the public domain. Here he explains how meetings are not confidential and the child or young person can avoid hassle by staying quiet:

> Yes, you soon learn that, if you're good, no-one takes any notice. It's hard to say what you want at meetings, it's safer to stay quiet. They don't keep it confidential and you can get into all sorts of hassle.

Eleven-year-old Kylie was concerned about the power of fostering agencies to remove children from their foster homes. Earlier in the interview she had explained how she had lived with other foster carers who she thought did not like her, but was happy and settled with her current foster family. Here she explains that she considers it should be up to the parents and children to decide if a child should stay with their foster family:

> **Interviewer:** What would you do to make fostering better for children?
>
> **Kylie:** Like the fostering agency, make it more like, if they wanted to stay there forever, and their parents wanted them to stay there forever, the fostering agency shouldn't be able to take them away.

The care-leavers in the discussion group had been involved with training foster carers and 22-year-old Charlotte explained one of the difficulties she identified in the way in which fostering agencies prepare carers to look after children and young people:

> They should train foster carers better, tell them what it's really like. They're scared to ask social workers, in case they don't get approved.

In summary, when meetings and reviews were reported by children this was usually in a negative way, for example they reminded some foster children that they were different. One respondent, Stephanie, mentioned a review as a place where problems might be resolved, but this had not helped her to obtain her outstanding clothing allowance as she had hoped. She was 'heard' but not 'listened to'. This has resonance with Hill *et al.*'s (2004) understanding that children's active participation is hampered by their status as people who are not reliable witnesses of their own experiences. Looked after children's formal participation in decision-making has been quite widely reported in the research literature (Shemmings 1996; Shier 2001; Thomas 2002), and there are typologies of participation that can be used to interpret levels of participation (Arnstein 1969; Hart 1992). Much of the formal 'participation' of looked after children in the review system that was reported could be considered as tokenistic.

Thomas and O'Kane's (1999) study of looked after children's involvement in review meetings found that children and young people adopted one of five distinct attitudes to the question of how much say children can expect to have. Thomas positioned looked after children's individual responses to decision-making processes as: assertive, dissatisfied, submissive, reasonable or avoidant positions (Thomas 2002). This typology assists in understanding differing responses, such as Andreas's avoidance of official decision-making meetings.

Three aspects of children's rights (UN 1989) were described earlier, in Chapter 2. Alderson and Morrow (2011) outlined models of participation derived from these rights: a protecting model, a providing model and a participant model. The participant model, which is typified by children sharing in the definition and solution of problems, is not apparent from these accounts, although it does appear in the policy literature (DfES 2004a, 2004b, 2006). The protecting or providing models of welfare service delivery appear more relevant to understandings of foster children's reports of their involvement in decision-making.

Trust

This sub-section concerns trust: the trust or mistrust expressed by children and young people who are dependent on the fostering system to provide them with a foster placement. Their reported concerns were frequently about living with strangers and the selection of foster carers. A marked theme in some reports of being fostered concerned whether or not children trusted that the organisation of fostering would look after them and provide them with good foster carers. The awareness of widely differing standards of foster homes was reported as arising from different sources: from the lived experience of being in different foster homes, from talking to foster siblings or from reports in the media. The understanding that some children can be harmed or harshly treated in foster care was mentioned by 12 of the 22 interview respondents, often those who said they were happy in their current home.

Trevor, aged 14, compared his own care to that of a foster boy he had seen a television programme about. He enjoyed the social aspects of his school, but not the lessons. Although I would have liked to have asked him about what he meant by a proper home, due to his learning disabilities and idiosyncratic communication mode my interview technique with him was not to ask probing questions, but to focus on understanding what he was telling me:

Interviewer: How can fostering be better for children?

Trevor: Yes. Like, give them more food. Some don't, this boy on the telly, he didn't get much food, went hospital… All kids who are fostered should go [to] proper homes. Some are, some not. This is fantastic. I say, all kids should get more food and no lessons. And more toys.

Seventeen-year-old Matthew also considered that some foster children were treated badly, attributing his placement in a good foster home as good fortune, rather than good judgement by social workers:

Interviewer: Is there anything that could be done to make fostering better for children?

Matthew: You can go somewhere and it's bad, like this kid [a foster child] that stayed here, he'd been somewhere and they got the dog to bite him, like. You can get hand-me-downs, like, say, the foster carer's got her own kids, she just gives you their clothes... And when kids and young people go into foster homes, they should be more careful, it shouldn't happen that children get bit by dogs, they should go more often. Like, it's alright here, but I'm just lucky.

Sixteen-year-old Stephanie had lived in several foster homes and had had changes of social worker, so had acquired some expert experience of being a looked after child gained during the last seven years, but she did not have much faith in care professionals:

I don't think it's really fostering, it's social services that needs to change, it's just the way they handle things, it's silly how long everything takes.

Stephanie's perceptive comments echo the earlier reports of Trevor and Matthew in illustrating how some children did not have trust that foster carers who were selected and monitored by social services could effectively ensure children's safety and well-being. Seventeen-year-old Bella qualified this position, in the discussion group, by explaining that, whilst children and young people could rely on foster carers to provide food and a bed for them, being safe and being protected was not a given, but was conditional on having good foster carers. This links with other data in this sub-section, where children and young people acknowledged that some foster carers exploit and abuse children. Bella told the group:

All you can say is that they will give you food and a bed. You don't know if it will be safe.

In summary, fostering was often reported and described by children and young people as a variable provision: they are not necessarily safe in a foster home, but if they are safe then this can be attributed to good luck, rather than good social work judgement. Many reported being aware that bad things can happen to children who are fostered: financial exploitation, physical abuse, poor provision of clothing or food. The anxiety about going to live with a new family, as reported in Chapter 5, can be better understood in the context of children's awareness that they will be dependent on strangers, strangers who may not necessarily be trusted to treat them well. This finding has some relationship to Sinclair *et al*.'s (2005) distinction between 'stranger' foster care and kinship care. Studies of children's views of the care system (Barnardo's 2008; Morgan 2006b; VCC 2003), as set out in Chapter 4, identified concerns of children being bullied and feeling unsafe, although these were largely related to either school or residential care settings.

How might fostering be improved?

Many children and young people who participated in my study made recommendations about how to improve fostering. Suggested improvements put forward by children and young people included less formal meetings with social workers and better access to social workers and birth relatives. Table 7.1 offers an overview of children's suggestions for improvements to fostering, followed by sub-sections of those themes that have not previously been considered, namely of enabling children not to be scared when they are first fostered or newly fostered, and better communication.

Table 7.1 Table of recommendations by children

Theme	Not being scared or worried	Better communication	Improved contact with birth parents	Fewer meetings
No. interview respondents	20	8	6	5

Theme	Fewer restrictions	Change the fostering system	Availability of social workers	More like own home
No. interview respondents	4	6	6	4

Fostering as a frightening experience

The most frequently cited response about how to improve fostering was for children not to be scared when they move. Twenty of the 22 children interviewed told me that they would advise new foster children not to be scared or afraid. This links to the preceding chapter, when children talked of being afraid and worried when first moving to a foster home. Four respondents said that children should be reassured or supported when they moved and were separated from their birth family. Thirteen-year-old James was one of the four interview respondents who considered that it would be helpful for children, when they first go into a foster home, to know that they would still see their birth parents:

Interviewer: If a child or a young person was about to live in a foster home, what advice would you give them?

James: Don't be scared. The people are usually really nice.

Interviewer: What might be helpful for them to know before they go there?

James: That they're still going to see their mum and dad, not to be scared.

Interviewer: ... Would you change anything about fostering?

James: Yes, less meetings and travelling to people. More help for people to settle in, social workers trying to make, persuade, people not to worry, to settle in like, to be more comfortable. Not just put them in straight away, what you do is like have a day like for a week, see them regularly to settle in. So it's not like with strangers.

James identified the potential discomfort at having to live with strangers and offers a sensible strategy to overcome this. As James's account explains, difficulties can be about missing your 'real' family.

Two members of the discussion group, when considering the finding that the interview sample children and young people advised new foster children not to be scared about going to live in a foster home, thought that this might offer a false sense of security to children. Twenty-two-year-old Charlotte considered that some children should be scared about moving:

Well, it's no good saying don't be scared, sometimes you should be scared, you don't know how it will be!

Most of the advice offered by the respondents to new foster children was about 'managing' their emotional state, not becoming overwhelmed: to be brave, to stay calm and not to worry or be scared. This was reflected in the interview data when 9-year-old Daniel gave the following advice for newly arrived foster children:

Don't really worry, try to be friendly, and try to get on with the other children, to mix with other people outside.

Seventeen-year-old Matthew said at interview that he thought little children who were newly fostered should be given a good present, to cheer them up. Being in a situation that you do not understand and trying to engage with this new environment can be eased by an act of generosity. This gives the child a positive experience, according to Matthew, who had witnessed the arrival of several new foster children, and acknowledged that they might have been initially intimidated or felt isolated at encountering three siblings who were already settled in the foster family:

> Yeah, when they first go, they should get like a present or something, like little kids, like my little sister, they should get given just one thing they really want, just to give them that start, so 'I'm in a foster home like, but'. See, I used to see people [new foster children] come in and they don't know what, they just used to see three [him and his siblings] from the same family, that's hard.

This advice was not just about recognising areas of difficulty for foster children, but also identified strategies that might assist in the resolution of those difficulties. Thomas and O'Kane's (1999) study identified differing stances used by looked after children in their attitude towards adult decision-making on their behalf, with some children acting assertively, but others submissively, when difficulties arose concerning placement, leisure activities, school and family contact. In considering the research question concerning the contributions that children can make to current understandings of the nature of fostering, peer advice could be a key answer. Peer advice is here understood as reflecting the standpoint of foster children and therefore includes difficulties about being fostered that might not yet be recognised by foster carers or social workers. This links with Andreas's earlier advice about meetings: 'it's safer to stay quiet'.

Better communication

Recommendations about how communication might be improved involved several issues: being properly informed by social workers and foster carers about important things, being listened to and keeping private issues private. As already noted, several children commented that it would be important to get to know a foster family before you went to live with them. 'Being listened to' by adults was a theme that ran through many of the children's accounts of whom they considered to be 'good foster carers' and 'good social workers'. Foster children's requests for better communication can be understood in the context of a lack of information about important decisions that had been made on their behalf. Eleven-year-old Beatrice explained how it felt to have to go and live with a family of strangers:

> It feels like you're all alone and you've got no-one to talk to but yourself.

Thirteen-year-old James explained how sensitive communication, when he wanted to know things about his past, had been of help:

Interviewer: Do you think that your foster carers help you when things are difficult?

James: If I have a problem or if I want to ask them something, like if I want to ask about the past, they answer it and if they don't know, they find out.

Interviewer: Does that worry you, not knowing about your past?

James: Sometimes I go through a phase of, I want to know why that happened, and I ask Mum [foster carer] and she finds out.

The lack of privacy for foster children, with detailed accounts of their behaviour reported back to their 'corporate parents' through formal communications, was described as problematic by some children. Records of children's reviews, for example, are sent not just to social workers, but also to social work managers, birth parents and increasingly other professionals such as teachers. Not understanding how information is shared, how information about looked after children moves from the private into the public domain, can have repercussions for children. Fifteen-year-old Alice had experienced information that she had confided to her carers being reported back to the social worker. This had then been taken up with her parents, who had clearly given Alice a 'hard time' for breaching family confidentiality. She advised new foster children to be more discreet:

> Not to tell foster parents their problems... Get to see their parents when they want, within reason, and that foster parents shouldn't report [to social workers] their foster children's parents, because then their parents give the kids a hard time.

In summary, many children reported feeling isolated and overwhelmed when they joined a foster home and they did not feel able to share those feelings with others. They have to negotiate relationships with the other three stakeholders in fostering: birth parents, foster carers and social workers. The children and young people are not always aware that these relationships are played out in the overlap domain, being both public and private relationships.

Chapter summary

Two aspects of children and young people's views of fostering services have been explored in this chapter: their evaluations of fostering services and their recommendations to improve those services. For many of the respondents, the practices designed to protect them were reported as somewhat irksome. For some children these processes made them feel different, uncomfortable or even anxious about other people finding out that they were fostered. They reported how meetings were preoccupied with discussing negative behaviour by children and young people, rather than about upholding children's rights by regulating the behaviour of adults. The checks that children and young people recommend to ensure their safety may differ from those that are currently in place, as do their reported concerns.

If foster children are aware that they can be taken away from the foster home because of a decision made by other people on their behalf, they considered this to be unfair. Although foster children appear to live in the private sphere of foster families, key decisions about their lives largely take place in the public sphere, at meetings and reviews. Overall, a pattern emerged of fostering reported by children to be a variable, almost haphazard service. The image of being fostered was not one that brought respect from other children. This was often exacerbated by confusion for children as to why they were fostered in the first place and therefore having no explanation to offer other children.

Most respondents had clear ideas about what might be done to improve fostering. Some of their recommendations had resonance with those in the research literature derived from children's views (Morgan and Lindsay 2006). Some of the recommendations were about areas identified in the fostering policy literature (DfES 2004a), for example young people from the discussion group wanting better matching of children to foster homes. This has similarity with policies aimed at providing a greater choice of placement.

Some of the restrictions imposed by public accountability seem to be resented by children, for example the relative lack of confidentiality when their 'private' concerns might be recorded and shared with others. The public accountability that children and young people recommended was more concerned with questions such as: Was their foster home a safe, supportive place for them? Did they have an opportunity to get to know and trust their carers before they had to live with them? Could they trust their carers and their social workers? Frequent visits and calls from social workers during the settling-in period were recommended by children. Following on from this, most children wanted a 'normal' family life with their foster family, or to quote 11-year-old Arthur, they did not want to be 'un-normal'. When social work assistance was required, they felt that prompt efficient responses should be forthcoming.

The use of a theoretical model which identified the intersection between the public sphere and the private sphere of being a foster child assisted understandings of the complex world of children and young people who are fostered. Looked after children depend on social services to provide them with a foster family placement. In Chapter 10 we explore the participation of looked after children further. Although the new *Care Planning, Placement and Case Review* (England) regulations of 2010 (DCSF 2010) position looked after children and young people as service users with an entitlement to an acceptable standard of provision, this was not apparent from the accounts in this chapter.

Part Three

Putting Children's Views into Practice

Chapter 8

Best Practice

Fostering is an innovative area of practice within which there are many celebrated examples of best practice. Indeed, one of the features of UK social work is that the standard of service is patchy, rather than of a generalist 'good enough' standard that one might expect in what is largely a well-regulated local government provision. One of the features of UK corporate parenting is the highly variable experiences of children and young people who are looked after, as we saw in the case studies in Chapter 1. The care system, however, is not one system: examples of good practice can be found in the voluntary and statutory sectors, in private fostering agencies and also from academic and research development. Innovative practice has often been grant funded as project work: this then either moves into specialist or mainstream provision, or disappears when the funding runs out.

The evidence from Sellick and Howell's (2003) *Knowledge Review* was that substantial developments have taken place in fostering practice. Many of those developments were funded by New Labour policy initiatives, such as Quality Protects. There are several excellent reviews of fostering and even good practice in fostering: Triseliotis *et al.* (2000), Sellick and Howell (2003) and Sinclair (2005), to name but a few. I have not sought to replicate those reviews here, but to focus on child-centred innovations.

In contrast to the earlier chapters, which focused on knowledge and research about fostering, this chapter moves on to explore examples of good social work practice. It, however, retains the main approach which I have adopted in this book as being informed by research evidence and children's rights, by selecting for inclusion examples of good, child-centred fostering practice. Rather than reviewing fostering practices in general, it sets out examples of effective, child-centred fostering practice in the areas of educational provision for looked after children and young people, support services, carers' recruitment, the participation of looked after children in fostering services, communication and also relationships with birth families.

What constitutes best child-centred practice in fostering?

It seems appropriate to use an understanding of child-centred practice that has been established by young people themselves. The Blueprint Project (VCC 2003), as discussed earlier, in Chapter 4, set out to consult looked after young people to establish what child-centred care should mean in practice. The report of that consultation project included the following list of the elements of child-centred care, which was compiled with young participants:

- The child should be at the centre of all decisions.
- Decisions should be kept focused on the child.
- The child should have some control and choice about his or her life.
- The child should have more choice than they do currently.
- The system should move at the child's pace.
- The child should always be seen and treated as an individual.
- The system should protect the child.
- Young people should be seen as important and listened to.
- Care should be about the child and their wishes, not the system and its priorities.
- A child-centred system involves seeing the world as the child sees it.
- Such a system prioritises treating the child with respect and valuing her or him.

This understanding relates centrally to the delivery or style of services, but also by implication to the design of services, for example by ensuring that there are sufficient foster placements for children and young people to have a choice about whether or not a placement move should also mean a neighbourhood and educational move.

As we shall go on to explore in Chapters 9, 10 and 11, child-centred good practice in most areas of fostering practice is difficult to achieve, with examples of good practice sometimes proving elusive to identify. The reasons for this are attributable to the culture clash within social work agencies, as set out in Chapter 2, where traditional, developmental approaches still dominate, with an emphasis on children as the objects of concern, rather than partners or service users. Perhaps the ambitious social policy moves, such as *Care Matters* (DfES 2006), have lacked resources and training necessary for such a culture change, or even that examples of good practice have lacked an efficient and consistent system of recording and dissemination. Despite these obstacles, there are nevertheless some commendable practice examples which have incorporated the views and messages of children and young people who are fostered.

Educational provision for looked after children and young people

A range of measures have been introduced to support better educational attainment by looked after young people. Following the Children and Young Person's Act 2008, all English and Welsh schools, from September 2009, were required to appoint a designated teacher to take responsibility for the educational outcomes of looked after children. The DCSF produced guidance in 2009, *Improving the Educational Attainment of Children in Care (Looked After Children)*, which sets out the different elements that should be in place to improve educational outcomes for looked after children (DCSF 2009b). These recommendations include appointing a 'Virtual School Head Teacher' to keep track of every looked after child, putting in place the appropriate provision to help each child attain their potential and overseeing the educational issues that social workers need to consider when making decisions about placement moves.

The Virtual School Head Teacher pilot project evaluation was completed in the summer of 2009. This initiative was judged to have demonstrated success in raising the profile and the educational attainment of all looked after children in the pilot districts. The use of private tutoring appeared to help many looked after children to reach their full potential. With the national roll-out of the programme, all local authorities are expected to have put a Virtual School Head Teacher in place in 2010. The *Care Matters* implementation programme introduced a personal educational allowance of up to £500 a year for any looked after child at risk of not reaching expected national levels of attainment (DCSF 2008). The widespread use of these allowances to provide individual tutoring for looked after children and young people could help them to overcome the educational gaps that are symptomatic of disruptions in learning.

Recognition and celebration of educational achievement can be a key motivator for children and young people. Wandsworth Children's Services have an annual formal awards ceremony for looked after children, the Keith Bridgman Achievement Awards for Education. Hosted by the mayor at a formal dinner in Wandsworth Town Hall, these awards aim to foster ambition, pride and self-esteem in looked after children and young people. This is particularly important for those children whose efforts are often marginalised in mainstream education. For children and young people in Wandsworth, being looked after doesn't mean that 'you couldn't make the effort, take your chances and succeed'. For some pupils it is these first educational steps of making an effort of returning to full-time education that is celebrated, but for some it is the achievement of a university degree. Young people formally accept their awards and make a speech in front of the audience about their own efforts and what it takes to stand up for themselves and realise their ambitions, often mentioning those who had helped and supported them. Good corporate parenting is important in improving educational outcomes!

Northumberland Local Authority, in common with several other authorities, have a specialist team to offer education support for looked after children and young people. The team aims to improve the educational attainment of Northumberland's looked after pupils. This is achieved in several ways: by prioritising and fast-tracking looked after children's school admissions wherever possible, by monitoring the performance of looked after children, by establishing and maintaining a network at local and strategic level to promote the education of looked after children and by advising and supporting schools and social care staff in matters relating to the education of looked after children. The establishment of Children's Trusts has supported joined-up service provision, a good foundation for implementing policies across two sectors such as education and welfare services.

Support services

Looked after childhoods are variable experiences, but many, at times, are marked by vulnerability and isolation. There is an emerging recognition that care-experienced children and young people have some expertise in helping to support each other. There are several successful groups run by care-leavers or older looked after children, usually with support from child participation officers, who actively provide services and support to other looked after children and young people. One of these is Kids In Care Together (KICT), which was set up in 2000 to give young people in the Norfolk care system a voice. The group has contributed in many areas and issues, ranging from sexual health meetings, speaking with the head of social services and attending Norfolk's annual education matters conference for the last five years, and have held workshops and performed a play. Now that Norfolk has a dedicated in-care council, the members of KICT applied for external funding to focus on support and socialising for young people in and out of care, and it even has its own website.

The Who Cares? Trust developed a secure online website called CareZone, which delivered a range of services for children in public care. In essence, CareZone was the closed website of a charitable trust used by looked after children in 37 different local authorities across the UK. CareZone was the first service of its kind, featuring child-focused technology, developed with continuous input from children: this resulted in service provision which they needed and wanted. Mindful of the vulnerability and isolation of many looked after children, it provided children with their own personal space for communicating and storing electronic files. Many foster children are moved around frequently and personal possessions can and do get lost in these moves. Access to the site was subject to several security measures, such as ownership of an electronic key fob which provided a constantly changing computer access code. All of those features were highly secure and accessed by young people in their own time using a Smart Card or fob and using individual log-on names, or pseudonyms. These measures were designed to protect vulnerable children from internet predators. In this way, CareZone provided a secure virtual space where children digitally stored items of personal value. The webmasters were online in real-time, so that they could offer support and guidance as requested, building trusted relationships with children over time. This made it easier for young people to ask for help if, and when, it was needed.

The services offered by CareZone aimed to reduce the sense of isolation experienced by many young people in care, as well as offering resources from a range of quality suppliers of information on health care, well-being and education technology. Some of the service providers were already known to many of the children; for example, a well-known teenage magazine 'agony aunt' responded to the 'problem page' part of the site. This was particularly helpful for looked after young people whose problems can be atypical and even more complex than those of teenagers in the general population. Interestingly the young people using this website asked for the name to be abbreviated to CZ: thus avoiding the social stigma of being 'in care' if using the site in a public place such as a library or school.

Sadly, plans to continue the project and expand to provide online educational provision for young people in secure accommodation and prisons had to be shelved due to funding issues. Virtual schooling provision has immense possibilities for those looked after children and young people who move frequently, are without a school place or are excluded from school. Although the lack of ongoing funding meant CareZone was closed down, it nevertheless provides an example of excellent exploitation of new technology to address the idiosyncratic difficulties encountered by many vulnerable young people who are looked after in public care. Some local authorities are now providing their own websites to support young people, for example the London Borough of Lambeth has the get to know (g2k) site, which offers support, information about looked after children's rights and a closed area only for those who are looked after.

Providing mentors for foster children is increasingly valued as a way of helping looked after children to achieve their goals. Skills acquired by care-experienced young people are becoming recognised as potentially useful in supporting those looked after young people who are facing difficulties, such as the transition to leaving care. Some care-experienced young people are getting involved in not just participation in service organisation, but also directly offering their services through mentoring schemes. In late 2010 funding was made available by the Department for Education aimed at providing 600 mentoring relationships for looked after children aged between 10 and 15, through 38 local projects. One project that provides mentoring is From Care 2 Work. This is a project delivered by Catch22, a national young person's charity previously known as the Rainer Foundation. In partnership with local care-leaving services, they aim to equip young people with the skills they need to find and keep and to help them with other parts of their life such as housing, relationships and staying clear of crime. As part of From Care 2 Work, care-experienced young people mentor looked after care-leavers. This scheme is proving popular with care-leavers, providing them with peer experience rather than adult expectations. Other young people who have recently successfully negotiated the same pathway can offer highly relevant and practical advice, such as how to get social workers to give you grants or how to get your friends to buy their own food without offending them.

The participation of looked after children in fostering services

Child-centred participation is here considered as an integral component of the design, monitoring and delivery of fostering services. It should not function as an added-on complexity, either delivered by external agencies or separate parts of fostering services that have yet to be incorporated into mainstream fostering services. However, many of the best practice consultations with children and young people are grant-funded projects, rather than mainstream provision. Chapter 10 deals exclusively with child participation, whereas this section focuses on some of the best practice examples within that area.

An exemplary nationwide consultation with looked after children and young people was carried out in the UK by the Blueprint Project (VCC 2003), as discussed earlier, in Chapter 3. The aim of the consultation was for young people to establish what child-centred care should mean in practice, as set out earlier in this chapter.

The first stage of the project was followed by work in six different local authorities to develop more child-centred approaches in practice. One of those projects was Kirklees Council's project to make their child-care reviews more child-centred, with children, young people and adults working together to make the looked after children's reviews more accessible to, and reflective of, the wishes of children and young people.

Several local authorities involve young people who are experienced in sharing their expertise to inform managers about care realities, to inform child-centred improvements and to recruit and train foster carers.

Cambridgeshire, for example, has a group for looked after children who contributed to spending reviews and who also helped to design staff training and information for other looked after children. Westminster made a video with children who were fostered talking about their experiences. This video was then used to inform foster carers, social workers and managers and local councillors about children's views.

'Leading Our Lives' is a project that aims to enable young people to have a genuine voice in discussions about their own future and about the services affecting them. It was set up by the Fostering Network with Big Lottery funding and has a website, photography and film projects and training for young people to become Fostering Panel Members. As a leading charity for everyone involved in fostering, Fostering Network aims to make life better for fostered children and young people and also for the families who care for them. As with some other projects, it merges the two groups of fostered young people and foster carers' own children and therefore is not just concerned with looked after young people, whose relative powerlessness can lead to a marginalisation of their interests.

Carers

One of the consistent, key messages from looked after children and young people has been that they want to stay in their own communities, go to their own school and be able to stay in touch with the people who are important to them, unless there are compelling safety concerns that mean that they must make a fresh start (Morgan 2006b). The lengthy foster carer selection processes, and the areas targeted from which to recruit carers, often mean that the available placements for children are a long way from their own communities. A child-centred approach would therefore be one which aims to recruit the majority of its carers from the same communities from which looked after children originate and to have flexible provision to meet the demand for foster places as the need arises to move children.

The Buckinghamshire Community Childminders Project uses a network of childminders to provide short-term and emergency placements for looked after children (Griffiths 2010a). It has 25 childminder carers, who have now looked after 500 children for periods of up to one month. Since being set up in 2005 with an original aim of providing respite care for children with a disability, the service now offers flexible care: overnight stays, short-term care or daycare, depending on the need. This is an example of shaping fostering services to fit local needs. Childminders have already been vetted to ensure they are able to care for children safely and in this instance have become an additional resource to meet the needs of looked after children and young people in their local communities.

Looked after children's messages about difference in religion and ethnicity between them and their carers appeared to centre on two issues. One was the potential stigma from perceived differences by others: in my own study, set out in Chapter 5, several trans-racially placed children discussed feeling uncomfortable about ethnic differences, for example feeling that the obvious differences between them and their carers compromised the confidentiality of their care status. The second message is about tolerance in the foster home for their own religion and ethnicity: being allowed to not hold religious beliefs or to keep their own beliefs or religion was also important, even if the foster family's beliefs were different (Morgan 2006c).

For many fostering agencies, there is a tension between placing children and young people quickly or waiting for suitable matches with a foster family in terms of individually assessed needs: gender, religion, ethnic origin, language, culture, disability and sexuality are all identified as needing to be appropriately accommodated in placements in the National Minimum Standards for Fostering, Standard 7.2 (DOH 2002). The National Standards, Standard 8.6, also require the carers of trans-racially placed children to receive additional training in order to offer appropriate care and positive understandings of individual cultural heritage. Other guidance from the UK government (DOH 1998) emphasises the need to avoid placement drift, if suitable placements are unavailable. This creates a tension for placement providers: having placements locally available for the sheer variety of cultures represented in some diverse populations is not resource effective and can lead to unused placements.

There are many examples going back to the 1970s of pro-active recruitment campaigns to provide foster carers from ethnic minorities and those with particular religious affiliations in order to offer children and young people a culturally appropriate upbringing. Some specialist fostering agencies target particular communities for foster carer recruitment and other local authorities have a long track record of searching for local carers who match the ethnicity and religions of many of their looked after children and young people. One example from the many excellent similar campaigns is Northamptonshire County Council's 'Somebody To Love' campaign, which is dedicated to finding foster carers and adoptive parents for black and minority ethnic children. Using such high-profile techniques as appeals on local radio, a message from a black celebrity care-leaver (Bruce Oldfield) and requesting a platform at local community events, Northamptonshire aims to reduce the waiting times for black and ethnic minority children needing long-term carers in their county. They are currently waiting three times longer to be placed than white children. Some of the barriers to the recruitment of non-English speakers are addressed by measures such as that employed by the London Borough of Lewisham, whose fostering website is available with Albanian, Mandarin, French, Somali, Tamil, Turkish and Vietnamese translation.

Recruiting child-centred carers from the same communities from which looked after children originate is clearly possible, but requires a pro-active, targeted approach from fostering agencies.

Contact with birth families

We know that the majority of children who are in public care for a period of their childhood return to their parents, or choose to return to them, in early adulthood (McCann 2006). Supporting contact between children and their parents, even following a period of separation, is not just about meeting the child's expressed needs, but can build resilience to the risk of social exclusion in adulthood.

Many looked after children and young people return home from care, but for others their relationships with birth relatives might be their only permanent relationships. A variety of problems, which are often inter-linked, are associated with a lower probability of rehabilitation to their birth family home: poverty, parental drug misuse or chronic mental illness, lone-parenthood, children with learning disabilities and so on. Children from such families are likely to remain longer in public care (Biehal 2006). Most looked after children and young people wish to retain contact with their relatives; in many instances this is clearly in their long-term interests, particularly for those who lack placement stability. Indicators of successful rehabilitation include: frequent parental visiting, a strong parent/child attachment, parental motivation, an absence of serious and persistent parenting problems, support to parents from social workers and purposeful, planned social work (Biehal 2006). There are, however, few examples of good practice to support children's contact with birth families.

A large private fostering agency in the Midlands provided care and services to the children directly and also indirectly through support to their foster carers. These services include an educational liaison officer, regular therapy sessions and a well-equipped contact centre where children meet their family and friends. This following comment by one social worker was typical:

> I have always found [the IFA] to be very child orientated and that basically their child care is good, they are able to provide a high level of support to all involved which benefits children.
>
> (Sellick and Connolly 1999, p.17)

The range and availability of additional services for children from well-funded private and independent fostering agencies might also be linked to their greater flexibility as they are not directly accountable bureaucratic organisations.

A peer consultation, *Every Voice Matters* (YSpeak 2006), was conducted by two care-experienced young people with children and young people in foster care and also the birth children of foster carers. The project was led by the Fostering Network, an umbrella foster care organisation. The project aimed to disseminate the findings widely to key decision makers within the participating local authorities, including senior managers, elected members and policy makers, as well as to the Fostering Network's members. They also considered if this model undertaken on a small scale could be replicated in the future with other children and young people in foster care.

The research methods were focus groups and survey questionnaires. Three focus groups were held, with 16 young people aged between 10 and 16 years old (eight girls and eight boys). Their care histories reflected a range of experiences from those who had only experienced one fostering placement to those with several changes of placement. Most of the birth sons and daughters of carers came from families who had a significant amount of fostering experience.

The survey questionnaire yielded 17 responses: nine from fostered children and young people and eight from birth sons and daughters. Looked after children and young people gave key messages about contact issues: the key messages were that contact is simply about keeping in touch with one's own family and loved ones. It is also complex because each child and young person has different wishes in relation to the contact they would like, frequency, the nature of it, venue and the decision-making process which can involve the social worker, foster carer and sometimes the court or other professionals who have a part in the care planning (YSpeak 2006).

All the participants expressed satisfaction with their contact visits: who they saw and their contact venue, especially if this was combined with an outing. They thought that informal contact worked well. Only one participant, who was settled in a long-term placement, had asked for contact to be reduced, because she felt uncomfortable as her mother was 'whispering to others'. All the other participants wanted increased contact time with their family. One participant wanted more information and reasons about why he had no contact with his parents. One boy (aged 14) expressed the view that there should be more experienced social workers to deal with complex contact issues, recognising that sometimes there is a need to work with both children and their families. Once a child or young person becomes looked after, he or she becomes the focus of social work attention and the family support is often withdrawn. This means that contact issues do not get resolved; there can be a tendency to ignore these or to just reduce or curtail problematic contact visits.

Best child-centred practice in contact visits can be seen to be an ongoing concern which requires skilled support. Flexible, informal contact that reflects the individual child's wishes and circumstances was reported by children and young people as what they appreciated. Even when there is no contact, children and young people want to understand the reasons for this.

Chapter summary

There are many excellent examples of child-centred practice in fostering. This chapter focused on best practice in the areas of educational provision for looked after children and young people, support services, carers' recruitment, the participation of looked after children in fostering services, communication and also contact with birth families. Many of these examples are small initiatives or projects, but some child-centred practice is now moving into mainstream fostering provision, such as specialist support for the education of looked after children.

Children's views have contributed to many improved practices in fostering, particularly where their experiences have been valued and efforts made to incorporate these into service delivery. One of the ironies of best practice in children's services is that it is often driven by policy initiatives or arises from the participation of looked after children which is facilitated by a separate part of children's services, by non-social workers. For many children's service agencies, child participation remains an added-on complexity that has largely yet to be incorporated into mainstream fostering services.

New technologies and the availability of project funding have also shaped some of the innovative best practice in the UK. The world wide web, for example, has particular usefulness for the engagement of socially excluded or isolated young people who often lack stable, secure social networks. Overall, this is an exciting time in fostering: there are many innovations and new opportunities available to enhance the experiences and reduce the vulnerabilities of children and young people who are fostered in the UK.

Chapter 9

How to Communicate with and Support Children who are Fostered

Introduction

Communication in social work practice is a complicated activity that demands sensitivity to people's current and past experiences, as Howe explains:

> the complex interplay between the past and the present, the psychological inside and the social outside, is the dance that practitioners have to understand if they are to make sense of what is going on and intervene appropriately and effectively. (Howe 1999, p.4)

For many children in public care their past life experiences have often been adverse, with the interplay between the past and present creating defensive barriers to ready communication. I would also argue that, when working with children and young people, the future is also likely to be of pressing concern, with much of the social work and care of looked after children centred on planning for their future.

In line with the child-centred approach to fostering, this chapter seeks to explore the ways in which children and young people in public care would like to be communicated with and to go on to consider how child-centred communication can best be achieved. Effective communication has three essential components: knowledge, a sense of purpose and skills. This chapter seeks to address those three areas in relation to looked after children and young people, beginning with communication knowledge. A sense of purpose is addressed through an exploration of child-centred communication with looked after children, setting out a model for child-centred practice in this area. The final section looks at communication skills, and the methods and tools needed to carry out child-centred communication.

Knowledge

There are several different areas of knowledge relevant to understanding communication with looked after children and young people: child development, a grasp of diverse childhoods, the frameworks of looked after childhoods and knowledge about how children and young people would like to be communicated with are some of the key components of child-centred communication with children and young people who are fostered.

A basic knowledge of child development is a core component of social work curricula, as looked at in Chapter 2. The essential issues for communication are a grasp of the three main stages of development prior to achieving adulthood: infancy (0–6 years), middle childhood (7–12 years) and adolescence (13–18 years). Each child follows their own unique pathway through childhood, with many highly individual differences in ability, cognition and culture influencing communication modes. However, a basic grasp of how children learn and develop is essential background knowledge.

Children and young people in foster care are far from a homogeneous group. The basis of child-centredness is about accommodating the needs and wishes of children and young people as unique individuals. Child-centred communication is therefore about accommodating children's own modes of preferred communication. Individual communication modes can be highly complex, for example the sometimes unique augmentative and assistive models of communication used by children and young people with sensory impairments (Lefevre 2010; Triangle 2009). Child-centredness involves a commitment to learning the requisite skills to enable children to communicate effectively. There are some occasions when assistance, such as the use of translators, might be more time effective than learning particular languages or communication skills. A wide range of skills is therefore needed in order to enable children to express their views.

For looked after children and young people, their status of being in public care shapes and constrains the ways in which well-meaning adults can communicate with them. The understanding of fostering as positioned in the overlap of public and private spheres (Goodyer 2009; Nutt 2006) blurs the boundary between the private lives of foster children with that of accountable public welfare services. This tension between the public and private, as set out in Chapter 2, overshadows much of the communication between children who are fostered and those who seek to care for them or support them. Being child-centred requires concerned adults to balance this tension between the private needs of children and the public accountability of working within children's services. Research with looked after children, as set out in Chapter 4, offers insights into how children learn the consequences of sharing what they had assumed to be confidential issues.

An aspect of communication with children and young people who are fostered is the unequal adult–child power relationship within which communication takes place. Effective dialogue with disaffected young people can be hard to achieve. It is argued by McLeod (2006) that much that appears unsuccessful in adult–child interactions can be understood in terms of power plays, with young people resisting the adult's agenda and trying to impose their own. True listening to disaffected young people requires time, so that a trusting relationship can be developed. It also demands an acceptance that the adult agenda may be flawed and a willingness to consider alternative possibilities (McLeod 2006).

In Chapters 4, 6 and 7 we explored some of the research evidence about children's views of the ways carers and social workers communicated with them. Despite the regulation and scrutiny of foster carers, it was apparent in many of the reports by children and young people that they did not feel safe in foster care. Many of them recognised that foster care was a place where children and young people could be abused. One of foster children's key communication needs must therefore be for them to be able to share any concerns with social workers, teachers and others and to know that their concerns will be listened to. Many of the children's views studies echoed that of Thomas and O'Kane (1998), who found that for children and young people their ideal social worker had good communication and listening skills, was understanding, helpful, caring, trustworthy and fair, had a positive personal style, was willing to advocate for children and would sometimes take them out. Concerns about social workers included that they visited at their own convenience or by arrangement with carers, meaning that children were not told when they were coming. They also needed to be more accessible to children by phone. These experiences of social workers being seen as good or bad appear widespread in the research literature.

Looked after children and young people's views of themselves as vulnerable in foster homes has implications not just for carers, but also for social workers who are responsible for monitoring their care and offering support. Many other professionals form part of the joined-up services received by looked after children and also have a responsibility towards them. Effective communication is essential in order for well-meaning adults, whether professionals, relatives or friends, to understand what is happening to children and young people who are fostered. Drawing on studies of what children wanted from their social workers (Butler and Williamson 1994; Goodyer 2009; Morgan 2006a; Thomas and O'Kane 1998), a key message was that they wanted workers who are good at explaining things and who are discreet and fair-minded: who talk about what children are good at, not just the bad things.

A key message from my research study, as set out in Chapter 5, was that better communication seems to involve several strands: being properly informed by social workers and foster carers about important things, being listened to and discretion: keeping private issues private and not embarrassing children and young people by breaking their confidences.

Within child safeguarding there have been ongoing concerns about social work communication with children. Inquiries have repeatedly catalogued the failure of individual social workers to form trusting relationships within which children could confide their abuse. Indeed some social workers have neglected even to speak with children at risk. My own research study (Goodyer 2009) revealed how children and young people who were fostered often talked about how, at times, they had felt unsafe in foster care. This places an obligation on professionals involved with looked after children and young people, not just visiting social workers, to provide opportunities for children to discuss their current well-being and any difficulties they might be experiencing.

The Children Act 1989 remains the key legislation for statutory care of looked after children. The new (DCSF 2010) *Care Planning, Placement and Case Review* guidance and regulations for implementing this Act recognises children's agency and strengthens their participation rights, as this excerpt below illustrates:

> Children should feel that they are active participants and engaged in the process when adults are trying to solve problems and make decisions about them. When plans are being made for the child's future, s/he is likely to feel less fearful if s/he understands what is happening and has been listened to from the beginning. Close involvement will make it more likely that s/he feels some ownership of what is happening and it may help him/her understand the purpose of services or other support being provided to him/her, his/her family and carer. Where a child has difficulty in expressing his/her wishes and feelings about any decisions being made about him/her, consideration must be given to securing the support of an advocate. (DCSF 2010: Section 1.10)

Munro argues that New Labour policies promoted managerialism at the expense of professionalism, which, through restricting social workers' time, autonomy and commitment to building relationships with children, acted to 'limit the power of social workers to respond to children's individual preferences…[and so] may paradoxically be creating obstacles to their empowerment' (Munro 2001, p.130).

To summarise, the frameworks of looked after childhoods can be seen to impact on effective communication in several key areas: power dynamics, accountability and privacy. The policy and regulatory frameworks surrounding social work in children's services place foster carers, social workers and other professionals in a dilemma: they are required to form trusting, confiding relationships with children, but also accurately to record and share those confidences. Skill and discretion are needed to balance these competing requirements.

A child-centred approach

Communication is a two-way process; it involves not just listening to, but also responding appropriately to, children's accounts of their experiences. A key component of child-centred communication must be that looked after children and young people feel able to share any concerns with social workers, teachers and others and to know that their concerns will be acted on.

Butler-Sloss, in her 1988 *Report of the Inquiry into Child Abuse in Cleveland*, made several recommendations about the need for effective communication with children. Butler-Sloss identified a need to:

- recognise and describe the extent of the problem (in that instance child sexual abuse)
- receive more accurate data of the abuse which is identified.

Her report also highlighted the danger that, in looking to the welfare of the children believed to be the victims of sexual abuse, the children themselves may be overlooked. She famously stated: 'The child is a person and not an object of concern' (Butler-Sloss 1988, p.245). This judgment remains the benchmark for social work communication with children in need.

Butler-Sloss's views were made in the context of child sexual abuse case hearings, when children's own accounts had been ignored, in some instances leading to miscarriages of justice. Her recommendations were the following:

- Professionals should recognise the need for adults to explain to children what is going on. Children are entitled to a proper explanation appropriate to their age, to be told why they are being taken away from home and given some idea of what is going to happen to them.

- Professionals should not make promises which cannot be kept to a child, and in the light of possible court proceedings should not promise a child that what is said in confidence can be kept in confidence.

- Professionals should always listen carefully to what the child has to say and take seriously what is said.

- Throughout the proceedings the views and wishes of the child, particularly as to what should happen to him/her, should be taken into consideration by the professionals involved with their problems.

- The views and wishes of the child should be placed before whichever court deals with the case. We do not, however, suggest that those wishes should predominate.

(Butler-Sloss 1988, p.245)

I would argue that these recommendations have a more general applicability, to include situations where plans are being made that could have a significant impact on children's lives.

Children and young people in the general population can also feel victimised and embarrassed, but usually have a far greater degree of stability, security and privacy than those who are looked after. Joined-up service provision and bureaucratic accountability have increasingly eroded the privacy of looked after children and young people. Sensitivity, respect for privacy and an awareness of how easily children and young people can be embarrassed or victimised are important components of communicating effectively with them.

Knowing what should remain private and what should be in the public domain of the records of looked after children is a delicate balancing act. The following examples of how children's confidences or circumstances become disclosed illustrate issues of concern that have been raised by foster children with me, either in my social work practice or during research with looked after young people.

Fifteen-year-old Keeli, a mixed-race girl who had previously lived with her white mother, was visited by her social worker in her new foster home three days after her arrival. She told the social worker that she liked it there, but the family ate Jamaican food which she was unused to and didn't really like. After a long conversation with her social worker in her bedroom, the social worker went downstairs into the kitchen and had a talk with the foster carer before leaving. As the front door shut, the foster carer stormed upstairs and shouted at Keeli for complaining about her cooking, saying things like 'Why did you tell her my food is foreign?', 'You've been messing around with white people too long, you've got no respect' and 'That's my livelihood you're wrecking'. The earlier warmth of the relationship disappeared overnight and Keeli learnt a harsh lesson about complaining about the foster carer. A little tact on the part of the social worker could have alleviated a lot of distress, rather than exacerbating Keeli's discomfort.

Thirteen-year-old Kevin had recommenced school after a long absence. On the first day he queued up with other pupils at his teacher's desk to get a password for the school computer. He was horrified when his turn came and, as his name was typed in, his care status and other personal information flashed up on the screen. Given the stigma and bullying that looked after children commonly report, this was a serious set-back for Kevin.

The understanding of fostering as positioned in the overlap of public and private spheres (Goodyer 2009; Nutt 2006) creates the intrusion of public scrutiny into the private lives of foster children. The public accountability of looked after childhoods, as currently regulated by local authorities in the UK, requires the recording and sharing of all information about looked after children and young people. This can create a tension with the private lives of foster families, the supportive and therapeutic intentions of social workers and counsellors and the emotional need for privacy of children and young people who are looked after. Many adolescents in the general population can be rather furtive in their communications with adults; this is at odds with the policies surrounding looked after children and young people, whose needs for privacy are largely ignored in the interests of establishing their wishes and feelings and the public accountability of services to them.

So, to summarise, the core features of a child-centred communication model are the following:

- All social workers responsible for looked after children should act in a reliable, child-centred way: the ad hoc provision of a 'good' social worker should be a right for looked after children.

- Social workers must attempt to form a trusting relationship with looked after children and young people.

- All looked after children and young people should have a social worker who keeps in regular contact with them and is accessible to them.

- Communication with looked after children and young people must be undertaken using modes of communication that are comfortable for them to use as individuals.

- Social workers should have a range of communication skills.

- Social workers should be able to accommodate individual modes of preferred communication, including the sometimes unique modes used.

- Carers should be good at explaining things to children.

- Children's privacy and confidences should be respected and treated with discretion, unless to do so would compromise their safety.

Skills: methods and tools

There is an acknowledgement that child-care professionals require skills in order more effectively to hear what young people have to tell us (McLeod 2006), but there are differing views on how that communication is understood. Colton, Sanders and Williams maintain that direct work with children 'operates at the interface between the world of children and the world of the adult' (Colton *et al.* 2001, p.61). Communicating with children effectively lies not just with being able to enter their world, but in the ability to bridge the divide, to translate between the two ways of understanding and communicating (Goodyer 2005). Ascertaining children's views is understood by Bannister as a three-way process: first building a rapport, then creating a safe space where feelings can be explored and, last, reassuring the child that their voice has been heard and their opinions will be considered (Bannister 2001). There appears to be a general consensus in communication literature that children's understandings differ from those of adults, with skill needed to bridge that divide. Also that children are far from an homogeneous group, with diversity within and between those from different social categories and families.

Talk in children's own social worlds is often intrinsic to other activities, such as play. Conversational analysis reveals how children's activities can be situated in the unfolding flow of talk-in-interaction (Hutchby 2002). Through the re-construction of a more relaxed social context, such as a shared activity, communication with children can be enhanced. What a child will discuss when involved in imaginative play with a responsive adult (Cattanach 2003) can be an improvement on the silent, anxious child often encountered in more traditional social work interviewing (Goodyer 2005). Good communication skills involving direct work or play are a means of stimulating discourse, and, in other contexts, are also used for clinical therapeutic purposes.

In selecting which communication method to use, it is usually appropriate to bear in mind the child's age, ethnicity and stage of development (Erikson 1982; Piaget 1936). The whole approach to communication with individual children can differ, often dependent on the age, capabilities and culture of the child. With younger children the use of props, such as teddy bears or puppets, can prove effective, whereas older children usually prefer a more factual approach. Streetwise children and young people can be more comfortable with indirect communication such as those involving the use of new technologies.

Activity-based work can facilitate communication both by process and by interpretations of the product (Thomas 2002). Drawing offers both an opportunity for building rapport with children not interested in a talking relationship, and can also provide a pictorial expression of a child's viewpoint. Paper-working and methods which avoid direct eye-contact can be more comfortable and less challenging for many children than traditional interviewing techniques. Flow charts, posters and water techniques can all be employed to convey ideas and information. For example, one water exercise involves the child pouring water from a jug into a glass which is wholly or partially covered with cling film. The water is symbolic of 'love and care', with the cling film representing one's defence systems, in this context acting as a barrier to the forming of close relationships. Children enjoy water play and can be engaged through this exercise to talk about their relationships and how past experiences can influence current relationships. To remain child-centred, it is usually appropriate to check with the child that the adult interpretation is accurate.

Christensen and James (2000) recognise that childhoods vary considerably and they employ a blank circle entitled 'my week', which children are encouraged to fill in and discuss. This method allows diversity and communality within a fixed conceptual form. Sitting down and drawing alongside children stimulates adult–child discussion quite effectively with most children. Particular methods are often employed for initiating discussion on a selected topic. For example, Banks (2002) recommends offering children a limited palette of coloured crayons and asking them to draw themselves, either alone or with their friends or their families; this can be a good starting point as a means of introducing the topic of ethnicity or of family issues.

Life-story work usually involves helping and supporting children to understand their own life history. This can involve using oral, video, pictorial and photographic methods as an alternative to the more orthodox 'scrap-book' method. For this work to be undertaken in a child-centred manner, the choice of language, the pace of the unfolding past history and the completed record must encompass the child's stage of development, personal choice, cultural identity and emotional status. The inherent concept of co-authoring a child's personal history gives the worker considerable responsibility in the selection and interpretation of appropriate relevant material (Goodyer 2005).

Mirror work, where you ask the child to look in a mirror and describe what they see, can be used effectively in situations where the worker establishes discourse with the child about identity or difference. More complex methods that involve mapping children's family and social networks can also work well, with children often enjoying the one-to-one attention.

Using technologies such as e-mail or texting, or newer ones like tweeting, blogging and social networking sites, enables social workers to keep in regular contact with children and young people, in a time-effective manner. One youth worker of my acquaintance texts all the young people she works with every Monday. 'Hope you have a good week. Good luck with the maths test/upcoming interview/seeing your dad'-type messages can help a young person to feel supported and they can help build a rapport with even quite disaffected or socially excluded young people. It also invites a response from young people when things are proving problematic for them.

Computers can facilitate communication in several ways: the use of internet chat-rooms, information posted on websites, adult–child shared use of software programs and electronic surveys are all emergent communication modes for working with children in a variety of disciplines. Although many children find the use of play materials to be of assistance in facilitating communication with child-care professionals, other children, notably those who are socially disengaged for reasons of sophistication, disability or adverse life experiences, may find the use of contemporary computer software more appealing. The enthusiastic and positive way that children have approached electronic communication has been noted in much of the relevant literature (Calam *et al.* 2000; Livingstone and Bober 2004; Watson, Calam and Jimmieson 2002).

Livingstone and Bober, in their 2004 study of the experiences of young people and their parents with internet use, found that approximately one-quarter of their 1,500 child participants identified some significant advantages to internet communication in the areas of privacy, confidence and intimacy. These perceptions held by children could potentially facilitate more effective communication with professionals, both child-care professionals and researchers.

Software has been used for work in highly emotive areas such as life-story work (Glasgow and Burns 2004) and determining sexual abuse (Steward and Steward 1996), but also in more routine areas like determining somatic levels for pain-relief, where a 'MacInterview' was used to enable children to pictorially locate pain and pain levels (Calam *et al.* 2000), and looked after children's reviews. In exploring the possibilities of using computers for psychiatric assessment and therapy, Calam *et al.* (2000) identify particular strengths in the use of computers for communicating with children. Some of these strengths are based around understandings that children feel comfortable and relatively empowered in their use of electronic communication. The greater mastery that children often have with computers can redress the usual power imbalance in their communication with adults. By providing a shared external focus, computers can also offer the opportunity for relieving eye-to-eye contact which can be experienced as intimidating by many children. Having some control over the pacing and nature of the responses available can afford the child a level of agency in the structured exploration of areas which the child may find difficult. By using a program which enabled children to delete, move or change responses, whilst simultaneously recording all the responses, an enriched data recording was achieved. A semi-structured interview format allowed the child participants opportunities for self-expression, with a gradual move from less emotive to more emotive material, building confidence gradually.

Other, more adult-centric strengths of using IT lie in the inclusive nature of using a medium which readily facilitates multi-language interviewing, without the need for an interpreter. By providing a range of speech files, including ethnic minority languages, sign language and age-appropriate language variations, interviewing literate children with a wide range of methods of communication is feasible (Calam *et al.* 2000). A computer-assisted interview is capable of helping children to share information in ways that conventional interviewing could not achieve and is considered to be particularly appropriate for children with learning or emotional difficulties and those with a disability which restricts their communication (Calam *et al.* 2000). The portability of laptop computers and the automatic, detailed recording of responses hold particular advantages for the child-care professional. The potential time-saving involved for researchers in not just recording data, but also having the data in an electronic form for quick and multiple methods of analysis, must make the emerging electronic methodology for interviewing and surveying with child research participants an attractive prospect.

There are those that argue that effective communication with children demands not just skills and techniques, but also core competencies. These competencies are identified by Lefevre as: knowledge about children and their communication modes, ethical commitments, and emotional and personal capacity (Lefevre 2010). The concept of ethical commitment, I would argue, individualises effective communication with children. A child-centred model of social work practice, or a rights-oriented model (Wilks 2011), is one that respects the rights of children and young people to the subjects of concern, not the objects.

Advocacy

Looked after children are vulnerable because of their dependency on public services to provide them with 'corporate parenting', and also because of their relative powerlessness to redress the situation when those public services prove unsatisfactory. Advocacy is increasingly important as a means of supporting the rights of looked after children and young people. Under the 2010 regulations for implementing the Children Act 1989, consideration must be given to securing the support of an advocate, where a child has difficulty in expressing his/her wishes and feelings about any decisions being made about him/her. In recognition of children's agency and to strengthen their participation rights, the new *Care Planning, Placement and Case Review* guidance and regulations (DCSF 2010) requires social workers to consider the use of advocates for children: 'Where a child has difficulty in expressing his/her wishes and feelings about any decisions being made about him/her, consideration must be given to securing the support of an advocate' (DCSF 2010: Section 1.10).

There are many different forms of advocacy, but Clarke (2003; cited in Boylan and Dalrymple 2009, p.79) identifies three forms suitable for work with children and young people:

1. issue-based advocacy – working with an individual on a particular issue in a task-centred manner

2. relationship-based advocacy – working with a child or young person in the long term and representing their wishes and feelings to others

3. general-issue advocacy – where an advocate campaigns on wider issues or supports groups to do so.

Each style of advocacy has its own skills set, and there are many differing understandings about advocacy, most of which include the following items. As a social work method with children and young people, these can be considered as the requisite capabilities and skills in order to advocate effectively for children and young people:

- being committed to children's rights
- being independent from service providers
- maintaining confidentiality, unless there is a risk of the child or young person being unsafe
- listening to young people, especially those who may have difficulty in communicating
- being able and willing to argue for a young person
- representing children and young people's wishes, interests, views and feelings clearly
- being reliable in dealings with children and young people.

Rights-oriented practice with children and young people is obviously a skilled activity and can be considered as a distinct form of communication with and on behalf of them.

Therapeutic communication

Another specialist form of communication is therapeutic communication. This is distinct from formal forms of therapeutic intervention, which are more usually carried out by qualified therapists within clinical governance. As a social work practitioner I advocated long and hard for psychological support for several young people who appeared distressed and vulnerable, but usually was faced with a reluctance by psychiatrists and psychologists to get involved with 'patients' who were not in a permanent placement. The premise of this reluctance is that children, like adults, need to feel secure before they can be assisted to resolve their psychological problems. Many looked after children, however, do not have a sense of emotional well-being and need support to cope with their lives as a vulnerable child or young person. The main skills involved in promoting resilience and also in problem-solving in a task-centred manner involve building trust in the worker as someone who is reliable, supportive and discreet.

Fraser, Kirby and Smokowski (1999) define resilience for vulnerable young people as:

- overcoming the odds – being successful despite exposure to high risk
- sustaining competence under pressure – adapting to high risk
- recovering from trauma – adjusting successfully to negative life events.

Particular sensitivity should be used to support communication with children and young people who have a fragile emotional status. Some agencies successfully use a therapeutic style intervention model with such young people; for example, Kohli and Mather (2003) describe once such agency, a youth asylum-seekers project, which threaded therapeutic support into the everyday lives of unaccompanied asylum seekers. Workers supported socially excluded and isolated young asylum seekers to find a plan to tackle their difficulties; often this was aiming for belonging in their new community. Workers dealt with the present first, then plans for the future and last they helped young people to deal with their often traumatic past.

Therapeutic communication is a skilled activity, often avoided because of the risk of causing further emotional distress. Sensitivity and reliability can be effective in minimising any potential harm. Avoidance of communicating with distressed looked after children has to be balanced against the risk of neglecting to offer appropriate support.

Chapter summary

In this chapter three components of child-centred communication in relation to looked after children and young people have been explored: knowledge, a sense of purpose and skills. The focus of knowledge about child-centred communication was informed by children's views of communication and a theoretical perspective that acknowledges the position of looked after children as both members of private families and also recipients of public welfare. The frameworks of looked after childhoods were seen to have an impact on effective communication in several key areas: power dynamics, accountability and privacy.

Next there was an exploration of how child-centred communication with looked after children operated, setting out a model for child-centred practice in this area. A commitment to rights-based practice and working within a child-centred practice model was described, along with the principles of child-centred practice. The sense of purpose for communication with children was approached from a rights-based approach perspective.

The final section looked at communication skills: the methods and tools needed to carry out child-centred communication. A range of skills and methods were described, from which practitioners can select the most appropriate way of communicating with individual looked after children or young people. The basics of advocacy and therapeutic communication with children were described.

These three areas of communication have been set out to provide the knowledge, sense of purpose and skills for communicating with looked after children in a way that moves on from a medical model that perceives children as objects of concern, towards a social model which recognises them as subjects of concern with rights to provision, protection, participation and even privacy!

Chapter 10

Participation

This chapter is concerned with participation, of children and young people who are looked after, in decision-making and also with how children and young people might influence fostering practices in a child-centred manner. That reflects two aspects of child-centred participation: the models of participation that are used and the practical ways or techniques that the aims of child-centredness can be achieved. These aspects are separately considered in this chapter, beginning with models of participation.

Listening to, hearing and acting on what children say are different activities (Roberts 2000). In the last chapter we explored communication skills: these are partly concerned with how to listen to children and really hear what it is that they are saying. There have always been people who have listened, or even heard what children have to say, but less often those who have acted on what has been heard. There are clear distinctions between collecting the views of children and listening to them in a responsive manner (McLeod 2006; Spicer and Evans 2006; Thomas 2005). Merely consulting children and young people, but not acting upon the views expressed by them to improve fostering services, does not constitute effective participation.

Models of participation

The models of participation that are used in organisations that deliver child-centred services draw on their own organisational culture, understandings of participation and the dynamics of child-centred working. Current understandings in the provision of children's services include concepts of service users as people who have a right to participate in the design, delivery and monitoring of social services provision. Models of participation in provision within social services have varied from those which are consumerist in origin to those which are concerned with power-sharing

(Beresford 2002; Hart 1992). Alderson and Morrow (2004), in a Barnardo's publication, identify three models of children's rights, 'the three Ps', broadly aligned to the underlying understandings about childhood:

- a Protecting model which perceives children to be victims or problems in need of protection

- a Providing model, which views children as dependants in need of services and other provisions

- a Participant model, where children are understood to be capable of expressing their own views and contributing to their communities – participants who are capable of sharing in the definition and solution of problems.

The existing culture and dynamics of children's services have often been reliant on understandings of their role in protecting and providing for vulnerable children. Child-centred participation, however, relies on understandings of children as capable of contributing to the design, delivery and monitoring of the services that they receive and also a commitment to children's rights. As has been demonstrated in earlier chapters of this book, although the legal and policy frameworks of UK looked after childhoods draw on the UNCRC (UN 1989) to promote children's participation in the services that impact on their lives, the more traditional understandings of childhood that are prevalent in social work can inhibit these aims.

Care Matters (DCSF 2009c) promotes the participation of looked after children and young people in their care arrangements. One method of facilitating improved participation is through Children in Care Councils (CiCCs), which *Care Matters* recommends should be set up in each UK local authority to offer looked after children a platform for airing their opinions on service provision. However, a ministerial review of the implementation of *Care Matters* found that a change of organisational culture is required to support the implementation of the new policies:

> There needs to be a change of culture in every local authority so that children are listened to more on key issues such as placement decisions; personal education plans; their health; and when and how they should leave care. The government is changing regulations to strengthen the role of independent reviewing officers (IROs) and asking all local authorities to set up Children in Care Councils (CiCCs). (DCSF 2009c)

Participation has also been defined in terms of the level of involvement in power-sharing, by such models as the 'ladder of participation' devised by Arnstein in 1969 and subsequently adapted by others for use with children (Hart 1992) and more specifically for use with children in care (Thoburn,

Lewis and Shemmings 1995). Criticisms of this approach centre around the difficulty in applying factors of significance to participation in the complex and continuing decision-making processes of looked after childhoods (Thomas and O'Kane 1999). Participation is instead viewed as an ongoing process, requiring a time investment for the preparation and support of participants and to enable children to learn the skills required for sustained and effective participation.

Children as service users who have a right to be consulted on policy issues and services that affect them are a relatively new concept, about which there is an emerging practice guidance for professionals. A 2005 Welsh Assembly competition for young people to sum up the meaning of participation was won by this definition: 'Participation means that it is my right to be involved in making decisions, planning and reviewing an action that might affect me. Having a voice, having a choice.'

Hart's (1992) analysis of the differing models of participatory involvement 'from tokenism to citizenship' views many existing models as decorative, placatory or manipulative, with full power-sharing and involvement by children as a rarely achieved goal. A typology of child participation in decision-making that divides approaches into clinical, bureaucratic and value-based (Welsby 1996) was used by Thomas and O'Kane (1999) in their data analysis of children involved in looked after children reviews. The clinical approach is perhaps a more traditional construct with children understood as being vulnerable to distress and as lacking in the capacity to fully participate in decision-making. The bureaucratic category has a resonance with the consumerist approach identified by Beresford (2002). The value-based approach is the one advocated by Welsby (1996), with the involvement of children regarded as valuable leading to better decisions, practice and outcomes. Thomas and O'Kane added a fourth category to this typology, 'cynical', where children are perceived as manipulative and spoilt, and as wanting power without wanting to take on the concomitant responsibilities. Foster carers were identified by Thomas and O'Kane as the main proponents of this cynical category.

An inclusive model for assessing children's own perspective of their involvement in decision-making meetings was devised by Shemmings and Shemmings (2001). The model involved collaboration with the professional to identify if the child's involvement extended to the following four areas:

1. seeing what is happening

2. being seen oneself

3. hearing what others are saying

4. being heard oneself.

Hart's ladder or typology of children's participation (Hart 1992), which was mentioned above and also explored earlier in Chapter 2 (see Figure 2.2), contains seven levels of participation. Taking the practice of looked after children and young people's involvement in their case reviews, the power dynamics involved in differing practices are illustrated below. There are obviously several caveats to be considered, such as the fact that not all young people would wish to chair their review or feel confident to do so. However, there are many confident, articulate looked after young people who feel frustrated by the way their reviews are currently managed.

Rung 1: Manipulation

Many social workers and other professionals have attended reviews when adults appear to coerce children and young people to contribute. These reviews are typically held in the school or foster home, irrespective of whether or not that is experienced as invasive or embarrassing for the child concerned. There is an agenda that meets adult and bureaucratic needs and the language and format are conducted professionally. Children's educational progress, family relationships, health issues and placement plans are routinely discussed. Inviting the child or young person to witness the professionally conducted meeting is the main contribution to participation.

Rung 2: Decoration

This style of review is broadly similar to the reviews described on the 'manipulative' rung above, but with some concessions such as a child-friendly consultation form used beforehand to gather children's views, or a part of the meeting conducted in child-appropriate language.

Rung 3: Tokenism

Tokenistic reviews typically consider an aspect of the child or young person's progress in a child-centred manner, such as 'Dionne will now explain why she wants to have more contact with her sister' or 'How can we make this work for Dionne?' The remaining parts of the review are conducted as in rung 1, but some non-contentious issues might be considered in a child-centred manner.

Rung 4: Assigned and informed

This style of review involves keeping children and young people fully informed about plans for their review, for example what will be discussed and who will be there. There are effective measures taken to ensure that children and young people understand what is happening at the review and are supported to attend what is essentially an adult-centric occasion.

Rung 5: Consulted and informed

This style of review seeks the views of children and young people about their lives and then plans for them after considering those views, but not necessarily 'hearing' them. One of the messages in Chapter 7 was how young people sometimes considered their reviews were preoccupied with discussions of any negative behaviour on their part, but failed to regulate the behaviour of adults towards them, for example if carers had failed to pass on their allowances.

Rung 6: Adult-initiated, shared decisions with young people

Although the review is organised by professionals and they set the agenda, serious attempts are made to ensure that children and young people's views are heard and taken on board in the decision-making. 'How can we ensure that Ahmed receives his back clothing allowance?' This is followed by a plan of action to ensure that the young person receives payment of the debt.

Rung 7: Young people lead and initiate action

Some London local authorities are now supporting young people to chair their own case reviews. Children and young people should be enabled to initiate review meetings, for example by contacting the review chairperson and explaining a valid reason to set a review. Invitations to the review, the agenda and venue can be discussed and agreed with the young person beforehand.

Rung 8: Young people and adults share decision-making

This would involve sharing key decisions as in rung 7, such as when to hold reviews, what issues are appropriate to be discussed in the public arena of case reviews and who should be invited. The shared decision-making can include what should be recorded, who would have access to the minutes and also a sharing of key decision-making such as planned moves and contact arrangements.

The use of Hart's typology can be helpful in guiding and evaluating participatory practices and, indeed, there are pockets of good practice in child participation throughout UK children's services. A truly participative agency, however, needs a widespread commitment to children's rights. This is sometimes achieved through building up networks: the London Borough of Newham runs training workshops on participation to help develop a network of participation workers furnished with these skills across the local authority and its partners.

Organisational culture of participation

Embedding a culture of children's participation within organisations which carry out their business within an inter-professional and managerial culture involves not just commitment and the reframing of existing approaches, but also the adoption of inclusive practices to facilitate children's involvement and best interests. Willow (2002), in her book *Participation in Practice*, brings together the lessons that the Children's Society learnt in their organisational transformation to achieving effective participation for children and young people. Identifying potential opportunities for young people to contribute, identifying people who can speed up progress, forming positive relationships with children and young people, disseminating best practice and having a plan of action to further children's participatory rights are all methods recommended by Willow as enabling organisational change. The National Children's Bureau (NCB) has similarly developed a handbook for facilitating young people's involvement in policy and the design, delivery and monitoring of services for children (Kirby *et al.* 2003). The NCB handbook also includes a section about facilitating the involvement of children with a disability.

One example of an organisation that supported some child-initiated reforms is the London Borough of Wandsworth Children's Services. Looked after children and young people in the borough reported that the orange form they were asked to fill out before reviews 'is rubbish': criticisms centred on questions that were too long and too vague, with no examples; they also complained that meetings were too long. Ten looked after young people worked with social workers to design a new consultation leaflet for use in their reviews. They made suggestions about how a new consultation form should look. One of the young people did a presentation to Wandsworth managers about how reviews could be improved, with ideas such as: let children speak first, make meetings shorter so that children can concentrate all the time and ask multiple choice questions such as 'How are you today?' with the answer: Great, Fine, OK, Had Better, Poor. All children then have to do is circle the appropriate answer, rather than worry about what is meant and how to write an answer.

Establishing the wishes and feelings of children and young people and incorporating these in the planning process is increasingly core to placement decision-making in private and public law court cases. There are many practitioners using direct social work methods, such as play therapy techniques and other child-friendly communication methods, to establish those wishes and feelings. However, there are ethical considerations about the consequences of those private feelings entering the public arena and becoming outside of children's control. Establishing wishes and feelings for the purposes of public care is rarely a confidential process, which can involve children in making decisions that have serious and long-reaching implications, about which they may be unaware. Some looked after children and young people are expected to make clear decisions about their living arrangements, even though this can mean voicing disloyal feelings about their parents. In McCann's research study about the parents of looked after children (McCann 2006), many birth parents had to acknowledge that their children did not want to return to them and this wish had been listened to in the care planning process, as this mother explains:

> She decided she didn't want to come and live with me…it was hard for me but she made a good choice I think. (Parent)
>
> *(McCann 2006, p.21)*

One area where formal decision-making about fostering takes place is at Fostering Panels, which manage much of the decision-making for each local authority and private fostering agency. They determine or ratify such issues as to whether long-term fostering is in the best interests of individual children or whether a child is appropriately matched with his or her carers, and also consider all applications for people to become foster carers. In addition, the panels identify any unmet needs for fostering and contribute to planning and service development. Typically membership consists of an appointed chair, vice-chair, several elected councillors, social workers and several independent panel members with fostering expertise. For some panels, the independent experts might be foster carers from a neighbouring local authority or, increasingly, a care-leaver from their own authority. Clearly there is considerable scope for looked after children and young people to participate in Fostering Panel activities and decision-making. There is also a requirement for all children's services to involve children and young people in decision-making, as set out in the Audit Commission's assessment criteria later in this chapter.

Participatory skills

A fresh approach to working requires not just a supplementary knowledge base, but may also require the acquisition of supplementary skills, both by practitioners and by children and young people. The core social work skills for working with children – responsivity, reliability, effective communication, accessibility and trustworthiness – are supplemented in participatory work by demonstrating a commitment to children's privacy, upholding children's rights, displaying advocacy skills and showing respect for children's views. Many of the key skills involved in facilitating young people's participation are communication skills, which we explored in Chapter 9. However, much of the work involved is with small groups of foster children, which might present a challenge to social workers who have previously worked in an individuated casework model. Many child participation workers come from a youth work or teaching background and have already developed group work skills.

Facilitating participation, as with other forms of communication, requires responsivity to the skills and competencies of the children and young people with whom one is working. Working with younger children and those with disabilities can demand a flexible, skilled approach, with a creative range of options available. Working in partnership with children and young people to resolve potential difficulties can prove effective. As with the Wandsworth looked after young people discussed above, if the forms are too complicated and boring, the service provider can always take children's views on board to provide a child-friendly alternative.

Many children and young people report that participation has offered them opportunities from which they have gained skills and confidence. Developing political insights into how organisations work, advocacy skills and feeling valued and empowered are all benefits from participation that are routinely reported by children and young people. Obviously, badly managed participatory experiences, such as those where children are not listened to or where communication modes do not generate inclusivity, can have a detrimental effect on children's well-being. A careful prior evaluation of how involvement will occur can minimise this risk. Some participatory involvement yields more tangible rewards, such as payment, gift vouchers or involvement in social events. At London South Bank University, some of the young people who contribute to the design and delivery of social work teaching joined our service-user involvement taught short course, which contributed to their GCSE Citizenship coursework.

Participatory responsibilities

Children's services have clear responsibilities to facilitate children's participation in fostering services: the Children Acts 1989 and 2004 and guidance and regulations of 2010, *Care Planning, Placement and Case Review* (DCSF 2010), all require services for children to consult and involve them in children's services. In the UK, the Audit Commission audits all the activities of local authorities, including the involvement of children and young people. Services which do not adequately consult and involve children are determined by the Audit Commission as failing to meet required UK public service standards. Good corporate parents, as other parents, are expected to listen to and communicate with their children. The Audit Commission's good practice assessment criteria set a benchmark for the involvement and participation of looked after children in their services. These criteria check whether or not:

- the service communicates effectively with looked after children using a range of methods
- staff have been trained and encouraged to listen to, and hear, looked after children and to support their active participation
- the key messages from children and young people are known at all levels of the service and by partners
- the views of looked after children contribute to shaping services and initiatives
- children with diverse needs and experiences are fully represented and supported in making their views known
- advocacy arrangements are available to looked after children
- the achievements of looked after children are celebrated according to their personal preferences.

(Audit Commission 2007)

These assessment criteria include such areas as determining whether or not the 'corporate parenting group' – directors, children's trust and service managers, social workers, residential staff, foster carers, schools, children's rights and participation officers – were aware of the views of looked after children. This measured benchmark is obviously set at a high, somewhat aspirational level: much work may need to be done for some children's services to meet this standard.

Chapter summary

Two aspects of child-centred participation have been discussed in this chapter: the models of participation that are used and the ways that the aims of child-centredness can be achieved through organisational cultures of participation. Effective participation in decision-making and influencing fostering practices involves an organisational commitment to children's rights. Most children's services trusts, authorities or agencies have some pockets of good practice. Some agencies have whole-heartedly embraced a new culture of child participation. Statutory frameworks require organisations who deliver children's services to support and enable them to participate in the design, delivery and monitoring of those services. Hart's ladder of participation was used to typify the differing ways in which children and young people might be involved in the routine reviews of their care.

Facilitating the participation of children and young people who are looked after is a skilled activity. As well as core communication skills, a commitment to children's privacy, upholding children's rights, displaying advocacy skills and showing respect for children's views were set out as prerequisites for facilitating effective participation by looked after children and young people.

In line with international human rights legislation such as the UNCRC (UN 1989), *Care Matters* (DfES 2006) and the new *Care Planning, Placement and Case Review* (England) regulations (DCSF 2010), which positions looked after children and young people as service users with an entitlement to an acceptable standard of provision, much remains to be done to facilitate their full participation in ensuring fostering services are child-centred. Children in Care Councils should be a key part of that process.

Chapter 11

Selecting Carers

This chapter explores the way in which foster carers are selected and considers whether or not the current selection process best meets the needs of looked after children and young people. This chapter begins with a summary of the messages from children's views studies about carers, including the findings from my own study as set out in Chapter 6. The main findings from studies that considered who makes a good carer are also summarised. Next the current selection process for foster carers is looked at and compared with other parenting assessments, both childminder assessments and assessments of the parents of children in need. The final section of the chapter explores the ways in which a more child-centred approach to the selection of foster care might be shaped.

Fostering practice is not usually led by research evidence; as Sellick and Thoburn point out below, it often relies on rhetoric for legitimation. 'Many of the certainties (in fostering literature), which are often cited, are actually value statements about what should be done, rather than what has been shown by research to be effective' (Sellick and Thoburn 2002, p.9).

In line with an evidence-based and child-centred approach to fostering, we begin with summarising the key messages from research about who makes a good carer for looked after children and young people. To recap from Chapter 4, the children's views research studies produced some interesting messages about carers. Children in Morgan's (2006c) study suggested that carers should respect and support their foster children's religion or lack of religion: it should be OK for children to keep their own religion or to have no religion. Children and young people should not have to change or acquire a religion to accommodate a foster family's beliefs (Morgan 2006c). Children and young people in that study also reported that they wanted to be able to trust and be trusted by their carers, preferably before they move to live with them. This finding has implications for the way in which moves to foster homes are undertaken, as well as for the selection of carers who are willing to invest time and effort in building relationships with children and young people before they join their family.

In Triseliotis *et al.*'s (1995) research study, most of the young people who were fostered said that they got on well with their foster carers. Being trusted and treated like the carers' own children was particularly valued. This study suggests that, for vulnerable young people, fostering can be hazardous. One-third of the young people were positive about their carers, one-third had mixed views and the remaining third had negative views. Those who were positive about their carers reported that personal qualities, such as being trusting, flexible and treated the same as the carers' birth children, had contributed to the success of their placement. The key messages from this study are about young people needing to be safe from abuse, near their own home and with carers who trusted them and were willing to accommodate a young person's social life.

In Chapter 6, findings from my own research indicated that children and young people who were fostered had clear views about the evaluation of carers and foster homes. Issues of trust or the absence of trust, fear of abuse, feelings of being vulnerable to abuse and financial exploitation were reported. These anxieties usually receded if the placement continued, but the key message in carer recruitment is that carers need to be trustworthy and capable of providing safety and reassurance to foster children, in order to alleviate these very real concerns. This research study also highlighted the different ways in which children and young people engaged with foster carers: some wanted substitute parents; others wanted less emotional involvement as they felt they clearly belonged to their birth parents. Some young people resisted emotional engagement with any adult and wished to keep carers at arm's length. These clear messages indicate a range of carers and foster homes are required: sensitivity to and an ability to accommodate the individual looked after child's circumstances, needs and wishes are important if that child is to progress in the placement. Most looked after children did attach particular importance to provisions made for them in the foster home and the carer's lifestyle. Whilst many appreciated factors such as outings and leisure opportunities, children in the same placements largely identified differing factors to those identified by their foster sibling, indicating that their evaluations were highly individual. This has implications for matching looked after children to appropriate placements.

Another area of concern for children was separation from birth siblings. Children's views studies illustrate the unique circumstances of each looked after child. Foster children's sibling relationships were found (Kosonen 1998) to be complex and highly individualised, with some suggestion that sibling relationships were more extreme for children who were fostered than for those in the general population. Some missed their siblings and felt worried and unsupported without them; others were largely relieved to be separated.

Unsurprisingly, moves away from schools, kinship, neighbourhood and social networks made children feel isolated and vulnerable (Brannen *et al.* 2000). *Care Matters* (DfES 2006) and the *Care Planning, Placement and Case Review* (England) regulations of 2010 (DCSF 2010) also emphasise the need to keep looked after children within their own local authority. A key message from children's views studies is that children and young people should maintain their social and neighbourhood networks, unless it is clearly not in their interests to do so, for example if they are at risk from violent relationships (Barnardo's 2008; Morgan 2006c).

Children and young people report how stigma, fears and a lack of even basic information can be part of looked after childhoods. They also report that they want to be 'normal', cared for and trusted. Studies reported that foster carers should trust young people like they would their own children (Goodyer 2009; VCC 2003). One of the key messages from foster children was that they wanted looked after childhoods to be normal, not a bureaucratically administered public welfare service where they have to wait months for requests about even basic information. This has implications for the selection and regulation of carers: children want carers to be able to make decisions about basic parenting. Carers also report that they want more autonomy in discharging their responsibilities (VCC 2003). This would require regulatory change to implement fully, since the Children Act 1989 emphasises a partnership between birth parents and local authorities in discharging their parental responsibilities for looked after children and young people.

Being vulnerable and bullied was identified by care-leavers as related to their care status: they had moved away from supportive relationships, had many more home and school moves and a lack of encouragement and support (Barnardo's 2008). Most care-leavers in the Barnardo's study had attended five schools, many had attended more than six schools and some had attended more than ten different schools. Over half had been bullied at school and believed that this was directly related to their care status. Care-leavers had reported an education that was relatively marked by disruption, a lack of support and stigma.

There are key research messages about carers' characteristics: as we saw in Chapter 3, carers who are warm, clear, firm, understanding and not easily put out are identified by Farmer and her colleagues as having lower-than-expected rates of placement breakdown (Farmer *et al.* 2004). An evidence-based approach to foster carer selection would suggest that recruiting carers with these qualities would enhance placement stability.

In moving away from a traditional social work approach to the selection and recruitment of foster carers, there are clear messages from the evidence base of fostering about the types of carers who might best meet the needs of looked after children and young people: those who can safely care for children, who are local to the child's own neighbourhood, who are calm, warm and firm, who are willing to build up a trusting relationship prior to placement and so on. None of these messages are particularly new or surprising, but they have yet to be used as the main selection criteria for foster carer selection.

The assessment of carers

Assessment is considered as a key social work activity and skill (GSCC 2002). It is also a theoretically informed process usually conducted with clearly defined goals. Assessment takes place within wider understandings of social work theory, with older social work assessment models reflecting the dominance of psycho-social models of social work (Goodyer 2008). In response to firm guidance arising from child safeguarding inquiries, many types of parenting assessments have become more evidence-based, moving away from the subjective, psycho-social assessment tools formerly employed. Evidence-based assessments tend to be more quantitative, objective tools for measuring people and their situations, and are attempting to move on from the more traditional, subjective assessments previously prevalent in social work.

In a review for the Social Care Institute for Excellence, Crisp and colleagues identified assessments of the suitability of carers as one of the six main purposes for which social work assessment was undertaken (Crisp *et al.* 2003). There are, however, several different types of carers, including both carers of vulnerable adults and those who care for children and young people. Children and families social work provides particular complexities for assessment, with the child being the object of concern, but the carers were often also assessed as to the adequacy of their parenting to meet the child's perceived needs. The Department of Health, in its *Framework for the Assessment for Children in Need* (DOH *et al.* 2000), previously known as the *Assessment Framework* but now modified as the *Common Assessment Framework* (DCSF 2007), sets out current principles for working with children and families. These principles require assessment work in child and family social work to:

- be child-centred
- be rooted in child development
- be ecological in its approach (i.e. looking at the whole child within his or her family and community networks)
- ensure equality of opportunity
- involve working with children and families

- build on strengths as well as identifying weaknesses
- be inter-agency in its approach to assessment and the provision of services
- be a continuing process, not a single event
- be carried out in parallel with other actions and provision of services
- be grounded in evidence-based knowledge.

(DOH *et al.* 2000)

There is an acknowledged shortage of foster carers, with a recent report (Clarke 2010) claiming that 10,000 more carers are needed to prevent the child placement system in the UK from collapsing. Clarke found that, in 2008–2009, 23 per cent of initial enquiries from prospective foster carers resulted in a formal application. Triseliotis *et al.* (2000) found that one in five enquiries resulted in a formal application. Three out of five of those applying, or 12 per cent of those who made the original enquiries, became foster carers. A high drop-out rate is therefore evident between initial enquiry to approval as a foster carer.

The Children Act 1989 requires local authorities to identify and provide services to 'children in need': those whose health and development would otherwise be significantly impaired, or who are disabled (Section 17(10)). All 'children in need' are assessed for services, using a framework assessment (DOH *et al.* 2000). Of these assessed children, many become looked after, whilst others can be determined as children in need of a protection plan or of local authority services. Framework assessments are required to be completed within seven days for the initial assessment and 35 days for a full, or core, assessment. There are three domains of these assessments: the needs of the child, the parental capacity to meet those needs, and the family and environmental factors. Assessments of parenting capacity link to the particular needs of the target child, taking into account dimensions such as disability, race and culture. This assessment, amongst other areas of concern, also screens for any harm the child might be suffering.

Recruiting, assessing and retaining foster carers is currently a complicated and lengthy process, largely determined by UK national policies, legislation and regulations, as briefly looked at in Chapter 1. The ubiquitous 'Form F', from the British Association for Adoption and Fostering (BAAF), is used to provide a standardised assessment tool for potential carers. The various sections of the completed form, together with the social worker's recommendation, are then considered by a Fostering Panel.

Foster carer assessments have yet to shift away from a psycho-social approach, although they have changed to encompass a skills component. Drawing on child development theories, the approach of Form F is preoccupied with the applicant's own parenting history, emotional well-being and their attitudes towards issues such as disability, challenging behaviour and minority cultures. Some aspects of this assessment draw on standards for the provision of children's services: applicants are required to be free of bigotry, supporters of difference and demonstrate that they lead a healthy lifestyle. Other aspects, such as being 'emotionally ready' to foster, draw on psychological concepts. One part of Form F is a lengthy portfolio of evidence of skills: these include some items such as ability to communicate with children, but also quite a lot of emphasis on local government 'political correctness' concerning the ability of carers to 'promote equality, diversity and rights of individuals and groups within society' (BAAF 2008: Form F 4B 2.3), to recognise the particular vulnerability of children with a disability to abuse and discrimination, and their ability to provide a standard of care that promotes healthy emotional, physical, sexual and intellectual development.

The process of selecting foster carers is a lengthy bureaucratic process, usually taking more than a year from an initial expression of interest before the placement of a looked after child or young person. In contrast, parenting assessments of birth parents have to be completed within 35 days, using the framework of assessment (DOH *et al.* 2000). These quicker framework assessments were introduced by statutory regulation, driven by public and media concerns about the lengthy and highly fraught assessments that were undertaken in child protection cases. Even in circumstances where favourable parental assessments were finally made, the children concerned had often been in public care for considerable periods of time before the assessments were completed.

Solihull Council has applied 'lean systems thinking' to the problem of lengthy foster carer recruitment processes (Griffiths 2010b). Mapping out the process in detail and then identifying any duplication, unnecessary delay and practices that were not required by fostering regulations enabled the usual 12-month recruitment process to be halved. The new system is a streamlined version of the previous one, but by 'smart thinking', which, for example, places applying for Criminal Record Bureau (CRB) checks at the beginning, rather than later as had previously occurred, considerable delays are avoided. This streamlined process meant twice as many local carers have been recruited by Solihull's own fostering workers, reducing the considerable expenditure on out-of-district private fostering agencies. Although apparently a finance-led solution, it delivered a child-centred solution by providing more local foster carers.

Families other than formally assessed foster carers have had success with caring for vulnerable children. As we saw in Chapter 8, the Buckinghamshire Community Childminders Project uses a network of childminders to provide short emergency placements for looked after children (Griffiths 2010a). This has the advantage of providing local, flexible temporary homes for children. The Gloucester childminders in this project are subject to the usual childminding assessments and receive four additional days' training a year. The route to being assessed and registered as a childminder is now via the Office for Standards in Education, Children's Services and Skills (Ofsted), which regulates and inspects childminders. Ofsted aim to register most childminders within three months of their application but there are several references which need to be taken before registration – a health check and CRB police check on the applicant and every other adult in their household. Their home will be inspected too, to ensure that it is a safe and suitable environment for children. Once registered, childminders must complete the first unit of the diploma course 'Home-based Childcare', which is usually available locally or by distance learning. They also have to complete a 12-hour Paediatric First Aid Course and gain a certificate. So, this is quite a different assessment process than that of foster carers – the main differences being focused on the child's experience as a part-time member of the household and about ensuring their safety.

There is considerable research evidence that kinship carers manage to achieve better placement stability and enable the children and young people they care for to achieve better outcomes than do foster carers (Broad 2001; Farmer and Moyers 2005).

To summarise, assessments of parenting and caring capacity vary; those used for assessing childminders, birth parents and kinship carers are usually considerably shorter than those used for foster carers. The evidence also indicates that kinship carers, despite many disadvantages, manage to offer greater stability to the children and young people for whom they care.

Discussion
As can be seen from the assessments of the parents of children in need and of kinship carers, effective parenting assessments can be undertaken within far shorter timescales than those currently used for the recruitment of foster carers. The current recruitment of foster carers can be considered to be pre-occupied with selecting emotionally 'healthy' parents who hold politically correct views. The main message from children and young people was about being safe: this suggests that robust screening out of potentially abusive carers should be a clear priority, as it is in all safeguarding assessments.

The success of kinship carers, who in comparison to foster carers largely live in impoverished circumstances such as over-crowded conditions and have poor educational achievements, indicates that factors such as generous accommodation are not particularly relevant. By focusing on shorter parenting assessments which are concerned with screening out potentially abusive carers, rather than trying to socially engineer particular types of foster carers, it could be possible to retain more of those applicants who express an interest in fostering. This would also offer a wider matching choice for placing individual children.

Some of the requirements often laid down by individual fostering agencies, such as each foster child having his or her own room and carers having to be non-smokers, further restricts the numbers of people in the general population from which carers can be selected. Whilst it is laudable to try to recruit the best possible carers, there is no evidence that this type of carer is particularly successful at bringing up looked after children. Children and young people who are looked after want normalcy; this can include less than desirable factors such as carers who smoke and live in over-crowded conditions, but not abusive or predatory carers. Farmer and Moyers (2005) found that personal characteristics were the best indicators of carers who could maintain placements. These qualities can be assessed effectively and quickly using psychometric questionnaires.

Finding placements in the same neighbourhoods from where looked after children come would offer them continuity of their existing networks. This can be important in avoiding social exclusion, as we explore further in the following chapter. A shorter carer's assessment period would also generate additional placements, both through the availability of placements with potential carers and also by lowering the drop-out rate of applicants.

Chapter summary

In this chapter it has been argued that current processes for the selection of foster carers are lengthy and intrusive, subjecting potential carers to a high level of scrutiny about many aspects of their lives and personal attitudes. The selection criteria have also been considered to be set at an unrealistically high standard, screening out, for example, the large percentage of the population who smoke or who cannot offer each child their own bedroom.

A child-centric approach to the selection of foster carers has been suggested, incorporating the key messages from research studies with children and young people who are fostered. Fresh selection criteria and a briefer assessment period could be key features in working with potential carers in the general population. The aim would be to find carers that could offer a safe, normal, stable and local substitute family home and upbringing to vulnerable children and young people.

Chapter 12

Conclusion
Towards Better Outcomes
for Foster Children

In this concluding chapter, we bring together the different aspects of foster care that have been explored in the earlier chapters. The aim is to look at the ways in which the various child-centred fostering practices set out in this book might contribute towards improving foster childhoods, beginning with an overview of the recent changes in policy and regulatory frameworks.

There is a well-documented, long-standing failure of looked after children to achieve in the same way as children in the general population (Farmer *et al.* 2007; Jackson and Thomas 1999). Whilst many care experiences are short term, these are often repeated short-term care episodes for the same child. Few looked after children, however, stay in the same foster home throughout their childhood and have a foster family which is a 'permanent base' (Sinclair *et al.* 2005). It is this piecemeal approach to corporate parenting that may contribute to disruption in looked after childhoods.

Although there has been widespread acceptance that current care systems fail to deliver good outcomes for looked after children, there is little consensus in the UK about the role of the care system. The following excerpt from the UK government's Department for Children, Schools and Families committee report for 2009 summarises their findings about the purpose of the care system (DCSF 2009c):

> Large variations in care populations around the country seem to indicate that there is no consensus about the role of care in services for vulnerable children. We are convinced that in some respects the potential of the care system to make a positive difference to children's lives is dismissed too readily, but we are also concerned by how widely the quality of children's experiences in care varies, and how uneven are the experiences

families have of support services prior to care. Children's services must have the tools to spot trouble in families at an early stage, and must be able to have confidence that the interventions at their disposal are of a high quality and will make a positive difference to families. We would like to envisage a care system that is seen not as a sanction against failing parents, nor as a catastrophe for children's future prospects, but as a way of supporting families that are under stress and not functioning well.

This shift in perception is only desirable if care is an integral part of a continuum of effective family support services, not an alternative to it. It is only justifiable if we are able to reassure parents that their child, when in care, will have stability and personalised attention rather than a life ruled by uncertainty and bureaucracy, will have access to all the health and therapeutic care that they need to enjoy life and develop into independent adults, will be protected from rather than exposed to risk of offending, and will not feel abandoned by children's services when they reach 16, or 18, or if they go into custody. There are some children in care who have all of this, and many more who have some of it, thanks to dedicated, compassionate carers and diligent local authorities. The question the Government must do more to answer is, how can we make sure that all looked-after children get all that they are entitled to expect from their time in care?

This recognition by the New Labour government of the 'uncertainty and bureaucracy' which can be experienced by some looked after children has fore-grounded much of the wholesale, recent changes set out in *Care Matters* (DfES 2006) and the *Care Planning, Placement and Case Review* (England) regulations of 2010 (DCSF 2010). The aim of the new regulations is to provide for a uniformly appropriate and child-centred upbringing for looked after children and young people, as the following excerpt explains:

> The regulations and guidance are designed to offer one coherent and easily accessible package relating to care planning and case review for looked after children. One of their central aims is to improve the clarity and consistency of the regulatory framework for looked-after children. Streamlining processes in this way increases the emphasis on more effective care planning and puts the child at the centre. (DCSF 2010)

These regulations contain an acknowledgement of the wide range of quality of corporate parenting that is currently experienced by looked after children in England and Wales. The aims are laudable, but it remains to be seen if the resources and training will be available to bring about the required culture change within children's services that would enable delivery of these goals.

The three case studies set out in Chapter 1 illustrated the wide variations of foster care experienced by looked after children and young people. The children and young people themselves have individualised care needs, many of which can only be fully understood by entering into a dialogue with them and in many cases also with their families and carers. As the UK government committee report quoted at the beginning of this chapter concludes, it is only through listening to children and young people's views about their services that a more uniform level of satisfactory care can be achieved. The following extract from that report highlights the importance of the voice of the child:

> there is the importance of the voice of the child. Only by setting more store by children's satisfaction with their care will we get closer to finding out how 'cared about' they really feel, how stable and secure their lives seem, and whether they have both opportunities and the support and encouragement needed to take them. Initiatives that seek to give children – collectively and individually – more say about their care must be specific, robust and enforceable. The variation currently apparent in services leads us to believe that more independent support is needed for children to express their views and have them listened to. (DCSF 2009c)

What are the barriers and drivers to achieving child-centred fostering practice? In Chapters 1 and 11, the shortage of carers from whom appropriate foster placements can be chosen for children and young people was identified as a major difficulty. The lack of choice contributes to unnecessary educational and social disruption for vulnerable children and young people and increases the potential for their social exclusion as young adults. Young people in the general population can benefit from the social capital of membership of neighbourhoods, communities and social networks to enhance their employability, to find accommodation and to provide emotional support and social opportunities. Young care-leavers who have experienced several moves may lack these social links, which increases their vulnerability to social exclusion and exploitation. Although keeping looked after children and young people within their local authority is now recognised as desirable, not least economically with local authority foster care placements costing less than out-of-area private placements, some local authorities are vast areas. Keeping school children within their own school catchment area would seem to be a far more child-centred goal!

In Chapter 2 I have argued that, rather than relying on attachment theory and an attribution of blame to deficits in pre-care early childhoods, a rights-based approach is concerned with how to ensure looked after children might benefit from the stable, consistent, caring parental relationships and the sense of belonging that are enjoyed by most children in the general UK population. The reliance of children's services on a medical, developmentally informed theoretical approach to foster care was identified as inhibiting a child-centred approach. The sociology of childhood, the sociology of health and Maslow's hierarchy of needs were set out as offering an alternative perspective for understanding fostering and looked after childhoods. This alternative perspective is more congruent with the recent policy and regulatory changes in fostering which are focused on children's rights.

In looking at the findings from fostering research in Chapter 3, Sinclair *et al.* suggested that foster care can often be considered 'impressive, when viewed as an isolated experience' (Sinclair *et al.* 2005, p.264), in offering looked after children a good, short-term experience of family life. It is when considered as part of a looked after childhood that the difficulties become apparent: even good short-term foster care can only offer 'a truncated, tantalizing and disrupted experience of family life' (Sinclair *et al.* 2005, p.264).

As we saw in Chapter 4, children and young people had clear messages about how fostering should be. They identified the bureaucracy of looked after childhoods as unnecessarily irksome. Much has been done, is being done and remains to be done in not just minimising the negative effects of these bureaucratic processes, but in ensuring widespread adoption of more effective processes. A lack of suitable carers to meet the assessed needs of individual children or sibling groups is a huge barrier to child-centred foster care. Streamlining and re-considering foster carer recruitment, as set out in Chapter 11, could make a serious contribution to improving this situation.

Chapter 5 explored children's views about moving to and between foster homes, from the author's own research study. A wide variety of types of moves were reported by foster children; many of these accounts illustrated how a relative lack of power, consultation and even basic information had been experienced. This highlights an ad hoc approach to best practice and a widespread disregard for children's rights: the rights of children to be consulted and informed about children's services were reported as being routinely ignored.

In Chapter 6, children's reports about living with foster carers were explored. Most of the children and young people reported favourable evaluations of their foster carers. Children's own agency and views about how they belonged, if at all, to their foster carers were clearly expressed.

The third and final part of the author's research study was reported in Chapter 7, which was concerned with children and young people's views about fostering services and systems. Again, there were clear messages about the good and not-so-good aspects of fostering: overall, a pattern emerged of fostering as a variable, almost haphazard service. Although children's private family live in foster care was provided as a public service, children wanted these foster childhoods to be as normal and private as possible and they were keen to avoid the stigma of being 'in care'. Accounts of their lack of privacy and confidentiality, and the way arrangements for them were made or neglected, reflected again a widespread disregard of their rights to such entitlements as a private family life.

As Chapter 8 demonstrated, there are many examples of excellent practice in corporate parenting in the UK. As the data from children's studies and other types of fostering research illustrated, as looked at in Chapters 3 and 4, there are also many looked after childhoods that are problematic, however. The care of younger children is generally more straightforward and their foster placements are less likely to break down (Sinclair 2005), but for older children there is less cause for complacency.

The three areas of communication, knowledge and sense of purpose and skills were explored in Chapter 9, with particular attention to confidentiality and privacy. Child-centred communication with looked after children was approached from a perspective that moves on from a medical model where children are perceived as objects of concern, towards a social model which recognises them as subjects of concern with rights to provision, protection and participation.

The participation of looked after children was explored in Chapter 10. In line with international human rights legislation such as the UNCRC (UN 1989), *Care Matters* (DfES 2006) and the new *Care Planning, Placement and Case Review* (England) regulations of 2010 (DCSF 2010), looked after children and young people are increasingly seen as service users with an entitlement to an acceptable standard of provision. There are many examples of good practice in this area; however, much remains to be done to facilitate their full participation in ensuring that all fostering services are child-centred.

The selection of foster carers was explored in the preceding chapter. An argument was made for moving towards a streamlined, evidence-based approach to these processes. Solihull Council has made improvements in the time it takes to assess potential carers, and other parenting and caring assessments were explored. Moving towards a child-centred approach to foster carer recruitment, instead of the current move towards the professionalisation of foster caring, could potentially ensure greater placement stability.

The bureaucracy of corporate parenting, the shortage of approved foster carers, the aspirational nature of full participation rights for looked after children and young people and a reliance on a theoretical approach to corporate parenting that fails to recognise children's rights have all been identified in this book as barriers to the achievement of delivering child-centred fostering practice.

Concluding the conclusion

Fostering is at the cusp of two paradigms. On the one hand lies the preoccupation with protecting and providing for 'vulnerable and damaged' children and young people, albeit in a piecemeal manner. On the other hand are the legal, policy and rights-based drivers forcing a shift towards a child-centred approach to fostering. The participation of children and young people in the design, delivery and monitoring of their care is key to the move towards a children's rights, accountable agenda. I have argued that it is not just the public service aspects of foster childhoods that need revision, but also the selection of the families with whom they live and the security, stability, normality and sense of belonging that looked after children might achieve within those homes. Using a Maslowian perspective, looked after children and young people require security, stability, consistent parental relationships and sense of belonging, as enjoyed by most UK children in the general population, if they are to have self-esteem and the focus to achieve and succeed into adulthood.

The seemingly arbitrary decision-making about where looked after children and young people live, which can result in dependence on the kindness of strangers, seems to be a distinctive feature of being a foster child. A reframing of foster care and a fresh, consistent approach to the provision, protection and participation of looked after children is the beginning of creating foster childhoods that enable children who experience them to have stability, love and a sense of entitled belonging. Much is being done towards these improvements, but much remains to be done: 11 per cent of looked after children and young people had three or more foster placements in the year 2009/10; this is clearly unacceptable. The aim of this book is to contribute to positive changes that will make being fostered a positive experience for all the children and young people in foster care.

The final message is from the looked after children and young people in the Blueprint Project, who produced key guidelines for adults working in children's services:

1. We have to focus on the child in everything we do.

2. The relationships children have are central to their well-being.

3. Children and young people are competent.

4. We need to create a better balance between working directly with children and all the other tasks which support this central activity.

(VCC 2003)

References

Abrahams, C. (1997) *NCH Action for Children, Making a Difference: Working with Women and Children Experiencing Domestic Violence.* London: National Children's Home.

Ainsworth, M., Blehar, M., Waters, E. and Wall, S. (1978) *Patterns of Attachment: A Psychological Study of the Strange Situation.* New York: Wiley.

Alanen, L. (1988) 'Rethinking childhood.' *Acta Sociologica 31*, 53–67.

Alderson, P. and Morrow, V. (2004) *Ethics, Social Research and Consulting with Children and Young People.* Ilford: Barnardo's.

Alderson, P. and Morrow, V. (2011) *The Ethics of Research with Children and Young People: A Practical Handbook.* London: Sage Publications.

Arnstein, S. (1969) 'A ladder of citizen participation.' *Journal of the American Institute of Planners 35*, 4 (July), 216–224.

Audit Commission (2007) *Best Value Performance Indicators Area for Investigation 7: Involving Children and Young People.* Available at www.audit-commission.gov.uk/localgov/audit/childrenandyoungpeople/lactoolkit/pages/areaforinvestigation7.aspx, accessed on 26 January 2011.

Aynsley-Green, A. (2006) 'Report to UK Parliament Human Rights Committee.' Parliamentary report no. 1278. London: The Stationery Office.

Banks, N. (2002) 'Mixed-Race Children and Families.' In K. Dwivedi (ed.) *Meeting the Needs of Ethnic Minority Children.* London: Jessica Kingsley Publishers.

Bannister, A. (2001) 'Entering the Child's World: Communicating with Children to Assess their Needs.' In J. Horwath (ed.) *The Child's World: Assessing Children in Need.* London: Jessica Kingsley Publishers.

Barnardo's (2008) *Failed by the System: The Views of Young Care Leavers on their Educational Experiences.* Available at www.barnardos.org.uk/failed_by_the_system_report.pdf, accessed on 22 March 2011.

Beek, M. and Schofield, G. (2004) *Providing a Secure Base in Long-Term Foster Care.* London: British Association for Adoption and Fostering.

Beresford, P. (2002) *Shaping our Lives.* London: Joseph Rowntree Foundation.

Berger, P. and Luckman, T. (1967) *The Social Construction of Reality.* Garden City, NJ: Doubleday Anchor.

Berridge, D. (1997) *Foster Care: A Research Review.* London: The Stationery Office.

Berridge, D. and Cleaver, H. (1987) *Foster Home Breakdown.* Oxford: Blackwell.

Biehal, N. (2006) *Reuniting Looked After Children with their Families.* York: John Rowntree Foundation.

Bowlby, J. (1969) *Attachment and Loss: Volume 1 Attachment.* London: Hogarth Press.

Boylan, J. and Dalrymple, J. (2009) *Understanding Advocacy for Children and Young People.* Maidenhead: Open University Press.

Brannen, J., Heptinstall, E. and Bhopal, K. (2000) *Connecting Children: Care and Family Life in Later Childhood.* London: Routledge.

British Association for Adoption and Fostering (BAAF) (2008) *Prospective Foster Carer Form F (England).* London: BAAF.

Broad, B. (2001) *Kinship Care: The Placement Choice for Children and Young People.* Russell House: Lyme Regis.

Broad, B. (2008) *Aspirations: The Views of Foster Children and their Carers.* London: The Adolescent and Children's Trust.

Broad, B., Hayes, R. and Rushforth, C. (2001) *Kith and Kin: Kinship Care for Vulnerable Young People.* York: Joseph Rowntree Foundation.

Buchanan, A. (1995) 'Young people's views on being looked after in out-of-home care under the Children Act 1989.' *Children and Youth Services Review 17,* 681–696.

Bullock, R. (2006) 'Can the corporate state parent?' *Adoption and Fostering 30,* 4, 6–19.

Butler, I. and Williamson, H. (1994) *Children Speak: Children, Trauma and Social Work.* London: NSPCC/Longman.

Butler-Sloss, L. (1988) *Report of the Inquiry into Child Abuse in Cleveland.* London: HMSO.

Calam, R., Cox, A.D., Glasgow, D.V., Jimmieson, P. and Groth Larsen, S. (2000) 'Assessment and therapy with children: Can computers help?' *Clinical Child Psychology and Psychiatry 5,* 329–343.

Cattanach, A. (2003) *An Introduction to Play Therapy.* Hove: Brunner Routledge.

Children Act (England and Wales) (1989) London: The Stationery Office.

Children Act (England and Wales) (2004) London: The Stationery Office.

Children and Young People's Unit (CYPU) (2001) *Learning to Listen: Core Principles for the Involvement of Children and Young People.* London: Department for Education and Skills.

Christensen, P. and James, A. (2000) 'Childhood Diversity and Communality.' In P. Christensen and A. James (eds) *Research with Children.* London: Falmer.

Clarke, H. (2010) *Bursting at the Seams: Impact on Fostering Services of the Rise of Children Going into Care 2009–10.* London: Fostering Network. Available at www.fostering.net/sites/www.fostering.net/files/resources/reports/bursting_at_the_seams.pdf, accessed on 22 March 2011.

Cleaver, H. (2000) *Fostering Family Contact: A Study of Children, Parents and Carers.* London: The Stationery Office.

Cleaver, H., Unell, I. and Aldgate, J. (1999) *Children's Needs: Parenting Capacity.* London: The Stationery Office.

Colton, M., Sanders, R. and Williams, M. (1988) 'Dimensions of substitute child-care: Foster and residential care practices compared.' *British Journal of Social Work 18,* 25–42.

Colton, M., Sanders, R. and Williams, M. (2001) *An Introduction to Working with Children.* Basingstoke: Palgrave Macmillan.

Corsaro, W. (2004) *The Sociology of Childhood* (2nd edn). London: Sage.

Crawford, K. and Walker, J. (2003) *Social Work and Human Development.* Exeter: Learning Matters Ltd.

Crisp, B., Anderson, M.R., Orme, J. and Green Lister, P. (2003) *SCIE Knowledge Review 1.* Bristol: The Policy Press.

Dahlberg, G., Moss, P. and Pence, A. (1999) *Beyond Quality in Early Childhood Education and Care: Postmodern Perspectives.* London: Routledge-Falmer.

Davis, J. and Edwards, R. (2004) 'Social inclusion, children and young people.' *Children and Society 18*, 2, 97–105.

Dencik, L. (1989) 'Growing up in the postmodern age: On the child's situation in the modern family, and on the position of the family in the modern welfare state.' *Acta Sociologica 32*, 2, 155–180.

Department for Children, Schools and Families (DCSF) (2007) *Common Assessment Framework.* London: The Stationery Office.

Department for Children, Schools and Families (DCSF) (2008) *Social Services Statistical Data.* London: The Stationery Office.

Department for Children, Schools and Families (DCSF) (2009a) *Safeguarding Children and Young People from Sexual Exploitation.* London: The Stationery Office.

Department for Children, Schools and Families (DCSF) (2009b) *Improving the Educational Attainment of Children in Care.* London: The Stationery Office.

Department for Children, Schools and Families (DCSF) (2009c) *Care Matters: Ministerial Stocktake Report 2009.* London: The Stationery Office.

Department for Children, Schools and Families (DCSF) (2010) *The Children Act 1989. Guidance and Regulations Volume 2: Care Planning, Placement and Case Review.* London: The Stationery Office.

Department for Education (DfE) (2010) 'Children looked after by local authorities in England (including adoption and care leavers): Year ending 31 March 2010.' Available at www.education.gov.uk/rsgateway/DB/SFR/s000960/index.shtml, accessed on 30 January 2011.

Department for Education and Skills (DfES) (2003) *Every Child Matters.* London: The Stationery Office.

Department for Education and Skills (DfES) (2004a) *Every Child Matters: The Next Steps.* London: The Stationery Office.

Department for Education and Skills (DfES) (2004b) *Choice Protects.* London: The Stationery Office.

Department for Education and Skills (DfES) (2006) *Care Matters: Transforming the Lives of Children and Young People in Care.* London: The Stationery Office.

Department of Health (DOH) (1998) *Modernising Social Services: Promoting Independence, Improving Protection, Raising Standards.* London: The Stationery Office.

Department of Health (DOH) (1999) *Requirements for Social Work Training.* London: The Stationery Office.

Department of Health (DOH) (2002) *Fostering Services: National Minimum Standards, Fostering Services Regulations.* London: The Stationery Office.

Department of Health (DOH), Department for Education and Employment (DfEE) and Home Office (2000) *Framework for the Assessment of Children in Need and their Families.* Norwich: The Stationery Office.

Durkheim, E. (1911) *The Elementary Forms of Religious Life.* New York: The Free Press.

Elliott, J. (2005) *Using Narrative in Social Research, Qualitative and Quantitative Approaches.* London: Sage.

Erikson, E. (1982) *The Life-Cycle Completed.* London: Norton.

Fahlberg V. (1991) *A Child's Journey through Placement* (1st edn). London: British Association for Adoption and Fostering.

Fahlberg, V. (2004) *A Child's Journey through Placement* (3rd edn). London: British Association for Adoption and Fostering.

Farmer, E. and Moyers, S. (2005) *Children Placed with Relatives and Friends.* Report to DfES. Bristol: Bristol University.

Farmer, E., Moyers, S. and Lipscombe, J. (2004) *Fostering Adolescents.* London: Jessica Kingsley Publishers.

Farmer, E., Selwyn, J., Quinton, D., Saunders, H. *et al.* (2007) *Children Placed with an Independent Foster Care Provider: Experiences and Progress.* Bristol: Hadley Centre for Adoption and Foster Care Studies, School for Policy Studies, University of Bristol.

Fox Harding, L. (1998) *Perspectives in Child Care Policy.* London: Longman.

Fraser, M.W., Kirby, L.D. and Smokowski, P.R. (1999) 'Risk and Resilience in Childhood.' In M.W. Fraser (ed.) *Risk and Resilience in Childhood: An Ecological Perspective.* Washington, DC: National Association of Social Workers.

General Social Care Council (GSCC) (2002) *Codes of Practice for Social Care Workers and Employers.* London: GSCC.

Gilligan, R. (2001) 'Promoting Positive Outcomes for Children in Need: The Assessment of Protective Factors.' In J. Howarth (ed.) *The Child's World.* London: Jessica Kingsley Publishers.

Glasgow, D. and Burns, R. (2004) 'Achieving Best Evidence: A Comparison of 3 Interview Strategies for Investigative Interviews in a Forensic Sample with Mild Learning Disabilities.' In C. Dale and L. Storey (eds) *Learning Disability and Offending.* Chichester: Nursing Praxis International.

Gonzales, N., Cauce, N., Friedman, R. and Mason, C. (1996) 'Family, peer, and neighborhood influences on academic achievement among African-American adolescents: One-year prospective effects.' *American Journal of Community Psychology 24*, June, 365–387.

Goodyer, A. (2005) 'Direct Work with Mixed-Race Children.' In T. Okitikpi (ed.) *Working with Mixed-Race Children.* Lyme Regis: Russell House.

Goodyer, A. (2008) 'Assessment.' In T. Okitikpi (ed.) *The Art of Social Work.* Lyme Regis: Russell House Publishing.

Goodyer, A. (2009) *Children's Views of Becoming and Being a Foster Child,* unpublished Phd thesis. London: The Institute of Education, University of London.

Goodyer, A. and Higgins, M. (2010) 'Stakeholder views about social work programme curricula.' *Journal of Practice Teaching and Learning 9*, 3, 92–110.

Greer, G. (1970) *The Female Eunuch.* London: MacGibbon and Kee.

Griffiths, J. (2010a) 'The work of the Buckinghamshire Community Childminders Network.' *Community Care,* 10 August.

Griffiths, J. (2010b) '"Just-in-time" car manufacturing system helps Solihull find foster carers.' *Community Care,* 25 November.

Guishard-Pine, J., McCall, S. and Hamilton, L. (2007) *Understanding Looked After Children.* London: Jessica Kingsley Publishers.

Harris, J.R. (1998) *The Nurture Assumption: Why Children Turn Out the Way They Do.* New York: Free Press.

Hart, R. (1992) *Children's Participation from Tokenism to Citizenship.* Florence: UNICEF Innocenti Research Centre.

Hill, M., Davis, J., Prout, A. and Tisdall, K. (2004) 'Moving the Participation Agenda Forwards.' *Children and Society 18*, 2 (April), 77–96.

Hollway, W. (2006) *The Capacity to Care: Gender and Ethical Subjectivity.* London and New York: Routledge.

Hollway, W., Lucey, H. and Phoenix, A. (eds) (2007) *Social Psychology Matters.* London: Open University Press.

Honey, P. and Mumford, A. (1992) *The Manual of Learning Styles* (3rd edn). Maidenhead: Peter Honey.

Howe, D. (1987) *An Introduction to Social Work Theory.* Aldershot: Community Care.

Howe, D. (1999) 'Psychosocial relationship-based theories for child and family social work.' *Child and Family Social Work 3,* 2, 161–169.

Hutchby, I. (2002) 'Resisting the incitement to talk in child counselling.' *Discourse Studies 4,* 147–168.

Jackson, S. and Thomas, N. (1999) *What Works in Creating Stability for Looked After Children.* Barkingside: Barnardo's.

James, A. and Prout, A. (1990) *Constructing and Reconstructing Childhood: Contemporary Issues in the Sociological Study of Childhood.* Basingstoke: Falmer Press.

James, A. and Prout, A. (1997) *Constructing and Reconstructing Childhood: Contemporary Issues in the Sociological Study of Childhood* (2nd edn). Basingstoke: Falmer Press.

James, A., Jenks, C. and Prout, A. (1998) *Theorizing Childhood.* Cambridge: Polity Press.

Jenks, C. (1996) *Childhood.* London: Routledge.

Kelly, G. (1995) 'Foster parents and long-term placements: Key findings from a Northern Ireland study.' *Children and Society 9,* 2, 19–29.

Kirby, P., Lanyon, C., Cronin, K. and Sinclair, R. (2003) *Building a Culture of Participation: Involving Children and Young People in Policy, Service Planning, Delivery and Evaluation.* Research report. Nottingham: Department for Education and Skills.

Kohli, R. and Mather, R. (2003) 'Promoting psychosocial well-being in unaccompanied asylum seeking young people in the United Kingdom.' *Child and Family Social Work 8,* 3, 201–212.

Kosonen, M. (1998) 'Foster Children's Sibling Relationships.' In R. Barn (ed.) *Exchanging Visions.* London: British Association for Adoption and Fostering.

Lefevre, M. (2010) *Teaching Communication Skills for Working with Children and Young People.* Bristol: The Policy Press.

Livingstone, S. and Bober, M. (2004) *UK Children Go On.* Available at http://eprints.lse.ac.uk/395/1/UKCGOsurveyreport.pdf, accessed on 23 May 2011.

McAuley, C. (1996) 'Children's Perspectives on Long-Term Foster Care.' In J. Aldgate and M. Hill (eds) *Child Welfare Services.* London: Jessica Kingsley Publishers.

McCann, J. (2006) *Working with Parents whose Children are Looked After.* London: National Children's Bureau.

McLeod, A. (2006) 'Respect or empowerment? Alternative understandings of "listening" in childcare social work.' *Adoption and Fostering 30,* 4, 43–52.

Maslow, A.H. (1970) *Motivation and Personality* (2nd edn). New York: Harper and Row.

Mayall, B. (1984) *Children's Childhood: Observed and Experienced.* London: Falmer.

Mayall, B. (1994) *Negotiating Health.* London: Cresswell.

Mayall, B. (1996) *Children, Health and the Social Order.* Maidenhead: Open University Press.

Mayall, B. (2002) *Towards a Sociology for Childhood.* Maidenhead: Open University Press.

Morgan, R. (2005) 'Foster-children and fostering.' *Childright 21,* 9, 17–18.

Morgan, R. (2006a) *About Social Workers: A Children's Views Report.* London: Commission for Social Care Inspection. Available at www.ofsted.gov.uk/Ofsted-home/Publications-and-research/Browse-all-by/Archive/Children-s-Rights-Directorate?query=Social+Workers&SearchSectionID=12&goButton=Search, accessed on 23 May 2011.

Morgan, R. (2006b) *Being Fostered: A National Survey of the Views of Foster Children, Foster Carers, and Birth Parents about Foster Care.* London: Commission for Social Care Inspection. Available at www.ofsted.gov.uk/Ofsted-home/Publications-and-research/Browse-all-by/Archive/Children-s-Rights-Directorate?query=Being+Fostered&SearchSectionID=12&goButton=Search, accessed on 23 May 2011.

Morgan, R. (2006c) *Placement, Decisions and Reviews.* London: Commission for Social Care Inspection. Available at www.ofsted.gov.uk/Ofsted-home/Publications-and-research/Browse-all-by/Archive/Children-s-Rights-Directorate?query=Placement%2C+Decisions+and+Reviews&SearchSectionID=12&goButton=Search, accessed on 23 May 2011.

Morgan, R. and Lindsay, M. (2006) *Young People's Views on Leaving Care: What Young People in, and Formerly in, Residential and Foster Care Think About Leaving Care. A Children's Rights Director Report.* London: Commission for Social Care Inspection. Available at www.ofsted.gov.uk/content/download/1410/10102/file/Young%20people%27s%20views%20on%20leaving%20care%20(PDF%20format).pdf, accessed on 30 June 2011.

Morris, S. and Wheatley, H. (1994) *Time to Listen: The Experiences of Young People in Foster and Residential Care.* London: ChildLine.

Munro, E. (2001) 'Empowering looked-after children.' *Child and Family Social Work 6,* 2, 129–137.

Nutt, L. (2006) *The Lives of Foster Carers: Private Sacrifices, Public Restrictions.* London: Routledge Press.

Oakley, A. (1974) *Housewife.* London: Allen Lane.

Ogilvie, K., Kirton, D. and Beecham, J. (2006) 'Fostercare training: Resources, payment and support.' *Adoption and Fostering 30,* 3, 6–17.

O'Kane, C. (2000) 'The Development of Participatory Techniques.' In P. Christensen and A. James (eds) *Research with Children.* London: Falmer.

Oliver, M. (1989) 'Disability and Dependency: A Creation of Industrial Societies.' In L. Barton (ed.) *Disability and Dependency.* London: Falmer.

Olsson, P., Folke, C. and Berkes, F. (2003) 'Adaptive co-management for building resilience in social-ecological systems.' *Environmental Management 1,* 34, 75–90.

Parsons, T. and Smelser, N.J. (1956) *Economy and Society.* New York: Free Press.

Payne, M. (1997) *Modern Social Work Theory.* Basingstoke: Palgrave Macmillan.

Penn, H. (2005) *Understanding Early Childhood: Issues and Controversies.* Buckingham: Open University Press.

Piaget, J. (1936) *Origins of Intelligence in the Child.* London: Routledge.

Pierson, J. and Thomas, M. (2002) *Collins Dictionary of Social Work.* Glasgow: HarperCollins.

Pithouse, A. and Crowley, A. (2007) 'Adults rule? Children, advocacy and complaints to social services.' *Children and Society 21,* 3, 201–214.

Pizzey, S. and Davis, J. (1996) *A Guide for Guardians Ad Litem in Public Law Proceedings under the Children Act.* London: The Stationery Office.

Prout, A. (2002) 'Introduction.' In C. Willow (ed.) *Participation in Practice: Children and Young People as Partners in Crime.* London: The Children's Society.

Quinton, D., Ruston, A., Dance, C. and Mayes, D. (1998) *Joining New Families: A Study of Adoption and Fostering in Middle Childhood.* Chichester: Wiley.

Qvortrup, J. (1987) 'Introduction: The sociology of childhood.' *International Journal of Sociology 17*, 3, 3–37.

Qvortrup, J. (1994) *Childhood Matters*. Aldershot: Avebury.

Reynolds, T. (2006) *Family Relationships, Caribbean Young People and Diasporic Identities*. Families and Social Capital Research Group working paper series. Available at www.lsbu.ac.uk/families/publications/pdfs/wp23.pdf, accessed on 12 December 2008.

Richards, R. and Tapsfield, R. (2003) *Funding Family and Friends Care: The Way Forward*. London: Family Rights Group.

Roberts, H. (2000) 'Listening to Children and Hearing Them.' In P. Christensen and A. James (eds) *Research with Children*. London: Falmer.

Rogoff, B. (2003) *The Cultural Nature of Human Development*. Oxford: Oxford University Press.

Rowe, J., Cain, H., Hundleby, M. and Keane, A. (1984) *Long-Term Foster Care*. London: Batsford.

Rowe, J., Hundleby, M. and Garnett, L. (1989) *Childcare Now: A Survey of Placement Patterns*. London: British Association for Adoption and Fostering.

Ruch, G., Turney, D. and Ward, A. (2010) *Relationship-Based Social Work: Getting to the Heart of Practice*. London: Jessica Kingsley Publishers.

Rutter, M. (1999) 'Resilience concepts and findings: Implications for family therapy.' *Journal for Family Therapy 21*, 119–144.

Scarman, L. (1986) House of Lords decision in *Gillick* v. *West Norfolk AHA* AC112.

Schofield, G. (2000) 'Parental responsibility and parenting: The needs of accommodated children in long-term foster care.' *Child and Family Law Quarterly 12*, 4, 345–362.

Schofield, G. (2003) *Part of the Family: Pathways through Foster Care*. London: British Agencies for Adoption and Fostering.

Schofield, G., Beek, M., Sargent, K. and Thoburn, J. (2000) *Growing Up in Foster Care*. London: British Association for Adoption and Fostering.

Sellick, C. (2006) 'From famine to feast: A review of the foster care research literature.' *Children and Society 20*, 1, 109–122.

Sellick, C. and Connolly, B. (1999) *A Description and Evaluation of the Work of Midland Care Associates*. Norwich: UEA Centre for the Study of the Child and Family.

Sellick, C. and Howell, D. (2003) *Social Care Institute for Excellence (SCIE) Knowledge Review Four. Innovative, Tried and Tested: A Review of Good Practice in Fostering*. London: SCIE.

Sellick, C. and Thoburn, J. (1996) *Family Placement Services*. London: British Association for Adoption and Fostering.

Sellick, C. and Thoburn, J. (2002) 'Family Placement Services.' In T. Newman, H. Roberts and D. McNeish (eds) *What Works for Children?* Buckingham: Open University Press.

Shaw, C. (1998) *Remember My Messages: The Experiences and Views of 2000 Children in Public Care in the UK*. London: The Who Cares? Trust.

Shemmings, D. (1996) *Involving Children in Child Protection Conferences: Research Findings from Two Child Protection Authorities*. Social Work Monographs 152, University of East London.

Shemmings, Y. and Shemmings, D. (2001) 'Empowering Children and Family Members to Participate in the Assessment Process.' In J. Horwath (ed.) *The Child's World: Assessing Children in Need*. London: Jessica Kingsley Publishers.

Shier, H. (2001) 'Pathways to participation: Openings, opportunities and obligations.' *Children and Society 15*, 2, 107–117.

Sinclair, I. (2005) *Fostering Now: Messages from Research*. London: Jessica Kingsley Publishers and Department of Health.

Sinclair, I., Baker, C., Wilson, K. and Gibbs, I. (2005) *Foster Children*. London: Jessica Kingsley Publishers.

Solberg, A. (1990) 'Negotiating Childhood: Changing Constructions of Norwegian Childhood.' In A. James and A. Prout (eds) *Constructing and Reconstructing Childhood: Contemporary Issues in the Sociological Study of Childhood*. Basingstoke: Falmer Press.

Solberg, A. and Vetsby, G. (1987) *The Working Life of Children*. Trondheim: Norwegian Centre of Child Research.

Spicer, N. and Evans, R. (2006) 'Developing children and young people's participation in strategic processes: The experience of the children's fund initiative.' *Social Policy and Society 5*, 2, 177–188.

Stacey, M. (1988) *The Sociology of Health and Healing*. London: Unwin.

Steward, D.S. and Steward, M.S. (1996) *Interviewing Young Children about Body Touch and Handling*. Monographs for the Society for Research in Child Development 61 (4–5, Serial No. 248).

Thoburn, J., Lewis, A. and Shemmings, D. (1995) *Paternalism or Partnership? Family Involvement in the Child Protection Process*. London: HMSO.

Thomas, C. and Beckford, V. with Murch, M. and Lowe, N. (1999) *Adopted Children Speaking*. London: British Association for Adoption and Fostering.

Thomas, N. (2002) *Children, Family and the State: Decision-Making and Child Participation*. Basingstoke: Macmillan.

Thomas, N. (2005) *Social Work with Young People in Care*. Basingstoke: Macmillan.

Thomas, N. and O'Kane, C. (1998) *Children and Decision Making: A Summary Report*. Swansea: International Centre for Childhood Studies, University of Wales, Swansea.

Thomas, N. and O'Kane, C. (1999) 'Experiences of decision-making in middle childhood: The example of children looked after by local authorities.' *Childhood 6*, 3, 369–387.

Thompson, N. (2006) *Anti-Discriminatory Practice* (4th edn). Basingstoke: Palgrave Macmillan.

Thorpe, R. (1980) 'The Experiences of Children and Parents Living Apart.' In J. Triseliotis (ed.) *New Developments in Adoption and Foster Care*. London: Jessica Kingsley Publishers.

Tisdall, K., Davis, J., Hill, M. and Prout, A. (2006) *Children, Young People and Social Inclusion: Participation for What?* Bristol: The Policy Press.

Toren, C. (1999) *Mind, Materiality and History: Explorations in Fijian Ethnography*. London: Routledge.

Townsend, P. (1981) 'The structured dependency of the elderly: A creation of social policy in the twentieth century.' *Ageing and Society 1*, 1, 5–28.

Triangle (2009) *Three Way Street*. Hove: Triangle.

Triseliotis, J. (2000) 'Intercountry adoption: Global trade or global gift?' *Adoption and Fostering 24*, 45–54.

Triseliotis, J., Borland, M. and Hill, M. (2000) *Delivering Foster Care*. London: British Association for Adoption and Fostering.

Triseliotis, J., Borland, M., Hill, M. and Lambert, L. (1995) *Teenagers and the Social Work Services*. London: HMSO.

Turpie, J. (2005) *The Participation of Looked After Children in Permanency Planning*. Unpublished PhD thesis, University of Edinburgh.

UK Children's Commissioners (2008) *UK Children's Commissioners' Report to UN Committee on the Rights of the Child*. London: 11 Million.

United Nations (UN) (1989) *Convention on the Rights of the Child (UNCRC)*. New York: United Nations.

Voice for the Child in Care (VCC) (2003) *Blueprint Project: A Blueprint for Child Centred Care*. London: VCC with National Children's Bureau (NCB).

Wagner, G. (1998) *Residential Care: A Positive Choice*. London: HMSO.

Warming, H. (2006) 'How do you know? You're not a foster child.' *Children, Youth and Environments 16*, 2, 1–9.

Waterhouse, S. (1997) *The Organisation of Fostering Services*. London: National Foster Care Association.

Watson, S., Calam, R. and Jimmieson, P. (2002) 'Can computers help in assessing children's postoperative pain? Initial validation of a computer assisted interview.' *European Journal of Anaesthesiology 19*, 510–516.

Welsby, J. (1996) 'A Voice in Their Own Lives.' In W. De Boer (ed.) *Children's Rights and Residential Care in International Perspective*. Amsterdam: Defence for Children International.

Wengraf, T. (2000) 'Uncovering the General from within the Particular.' In P. Chamberlayne, J. Bornat and T. Wengraf (eds) *The Turn to Biographical Methods in Social Science*. London: Routledge.

Wilks, T. (2011) 'The Ethics of Using Power in Practice.' In T. Okitikpi (ed.) *Social Control and the Use of Power in Social Work with Children and Families*. Lyme Regis: Russell House.

Willow, C. (2002) *Participation in Practice*. London: The Children's Society.

Wilson, K., Sinclair, I., Taylor, C., Pithouse, A. and Sellick, C. (2004) *Social Care Institute for Excellence, Knowledge Review 5: Fostering Success*. Bristol: The Policy Press.

Winter, K. (2006) 'Widening our knowledge concerning young looked after children: The case for research using sociological models of childhood.' *Child and Family Social Work 11*, 1, 55–64.

Woodhead, M. (1997) 'Psychology and the Cultural Construction of Children's Needs.' In A. James and A. Prout (eds) *Constructing and Reconstructing Childhood: Contemporary Issues in the Sociological Study of Childhood*. Basingstoke: Falmer Press.

Wyness, M. (2006) *Childhood and Society: An Introduction to the Sociology of Childhood*. Basingstoke: Palgrave Macmillan.

YSpeak (2006) *Every Voice Matters*. Available at www.fostering.net/resources/reports/every-voice-matters, accessed on 23 May 2011.

Subject Index

Author Index